HARVEST Your Wealth

Cash In ~ Cash Out

Exit Essentials For Your Business

The Business Wealth Crisis

"A calculated, adjustable exit strategy puts business owners in the ideal position to face the unexpected, whether the event is fortuitous, from a disagreement to a death or divorce, or providential such as an off-market offer for the business.

An exit strategy enables business owners to take control of the selling process and ensure superfluous problems or delays are not encountered, which can reduce the price a business can fetch."
Michaela McNamara ~ Editor-n-Chief of Business Review Australia

"the difference between greatness and mediocrity, mediocrity and millions, spectacular and pathetic performance is how well you use your time, your opportunities, your efforts, your resources and your assets."
Jay Abraham ~ The $9.4 Billion Dollar Man

"A business that operates successfully and profitably without relying on the day-to-day efforts of the owner is something worth paying for."
Paul Banister ~ Director of Tax for Grant Thornton Australia

"A well-developed exit strategy also allows you to maximize the value of the business by enabling you to address the drivers that impact the price of the sale and can manage the expectations of partners, colleagues and family."
Joseph Bridger ~ Partner Corporate Transactions, Pitcher Partners

HARVEST
Your Wealth

Cash In ~ Cash Out

Exit Essentials For Your Business

Kerri Salls

This Way Out Press
Framingham, Massachusetts

This Way Out Press
HARVESET Your Wealth – Exit Essentials For Your Business

ISBN 978-0-9885915-0-9

First edition

Additional copies of HARVEST Your Wealth may be purchased at www.thiswayoutgroup.com

For information please contact:

This Way Out Group LLC
1257 Worcester Rd #203
Framingham, Massachusetts, 01701
508.820.3322

Book cover concept, design and graphics created by Sergio Garcia of URBusinessNetwork.

Printed in the United States of America

Dedication

To my Dad who modeled entrepreneurship his whole life. He showed me what's possible for you, your family, your team and your business when you plan your exit from the outset of your business.

To my sons who give me purpose.

Table of Contents

PART III Foundations for Growth and Value 91

PLAN 91

STAGE 122

Preface

You are a business owner your goal beyond income is to build your company to produce wealth.

You envision, strategize and execute to achieve the promise you made to your family and yourself.

You are building your legacy now with an exit plan to fulfill those promises.

You must secure your transition to reinvention on your terms and on your timeline.

You hold in your hands a powerful book. It is your guide, your plan, and your advisor to structure a clean, solid and profitable business exit strategy.

Introduction

My father was not your straight A student at Philip Exeter Academy, Harvard University or Babson College of Entrepreneurship. He was having too much fun, making things happen. In business, he was an astute strategic visionary who recognized trends in the marketplace and opportunities and was always at the cutting edge.

At age 33, my father left his corporate position in Boston and launched his own business with two partners in 1960. He had four pre-school children at home. He didn't use the four of us as an excuse not to start his business, but as the reason he must start his own business.

He loved what he did. He looked forward to getting up to go to work every day. The business grew to 5 offices blanketing the region, received many regional and national accolades, awards, features and interviews, etc. He fulfilled every goal he had set for the business.

In 1982 my father was diagnosed with cancer. By 1984, he was too jaundiced to appear at the office or be seen by clients. That's when he invoked the buy-out clause in their partnership agreement. Here's the point of my story. He had had the foresight to have an exit strategy established from the day they opened their doors 25 years prior *when he was young and healthy*.

He and his part-time partners each knew the others would be their successors if anything unforeseen should happen. He never dreamed he would be the one to have to invoke that paragraph of their business plan, certainly not for terminal cancer at age 54. But when he needed it, he could and did. His partners bought him out and the business continued without a hiccup.

It was a simple quick congenial meeting at the lawyer's office to sign a few documents and it was done. My mother's financial future was secured, and the business continued with essentially no strategic impact on customers, employees or profits.

With that example, I assumed that all business sales/exits were as straightforward and smooth as buying or selling a house or a car. Only when I started consulting to technology and service firms a few years later, in 1988, did I begin to realize that most business owners never think about their exit.

With the hindsight of my father's successful exit, and working with hundreds of business owners, I know what's possible even for a small business owner consumed by day-to-day operations.

That's the business owner who needs to start exit planning now. That's who this book is written for.

This process could take years and it does involve many components.

Just as your business can change, from the product mix, markets, marketing channels to management; so too can your exit strategy change. You need to review it and revise it as often as necessary, at least annually.

Why You Need This Book

Most owners and entrepreneurs never get to liquidate the assets in their business. Here's "why":

- Ninety-five percent do not plan how or when they'll get out. They postpone, procrastinate, avoid and deny the need to plan their exit. We'll get into more statistics later.
- Without a contingency plan, the family often cannot pick up the pieces and keep the business viable.
- Without a succession plan – a buyer can't see the value in the business without you.
- With all the effort that went into starting and building the business, there was no forethought on how to get out, how to get their wealth out, how to transition to their reinvention.
- Even with a team of expert advisors, the owner has never had a joint discussion with all of them to develop an integrated selling strategy.

When it comes to your exit essentials, let me tell you the questions I would ask and the questions I doubt if you would think you need to ask that you should. The questions to ask and answer are extensive. Answer them as you read to benefit your business.

In my whitepaper: _Don't Murder Your Business_, I raised awareness of the four key flaws that challenge all owners. I also identified three broad areas of blinders that CEOS/owners/leaders put on themselves, often without recognizing them. I won't repeat them here, but you can get a copy of this whitepaper at www.thiswayoutgroup.com.

However, it is essential for you to recognize your own excuses that prevent you from doing what you need to do now to get what you want when you exit.

Not taking action can be as restricting as settling into habits you can't break.

Inaction can become a general habit that causes you to:

- Leave unfinished projects lying around your office?
- Do meaningless busy-work instead of important money-making projects?
- Wait until the last minute (or even later) to file your taxes?
- Sometimes pay bills late?
- Show up for important meetings after the program starts?
- Make a to-do list, and then ignore it?
- Intend to make a budget and a marketing plan for the year and never get around to it?
- Set annual and long-term goals that would prepare the business for your exit, and never use them in operational decision-making?

The question is not what to do.
You already know that.
It's actually doing it that's the problem.

The typical excuses for not doing what you know you should, even if you're highly motivated, even if you want something very badly, and even if you know exactly what you need to do to get it; if you've got these internal circumstances operating, you AREN'T going to be able to do it.

The 10 of the most common excuses for inaction, include

Excuse #1: *"I'm too stressed out."*
Excuse #2: *"I don't believe I can."*
Excuse #3: *"I don't have the time."*
Excuse #4: *"I don't have the energy."*
Excuse #5: *"I'm too emotional."*
Excuse #6: *"I'll always be the way I am."*
Excuse #7: *"I'm afraid I'll make a mistake."*
Excuse #8: *"I'm too sick."*
Excuse #9: *"I'm too skeptical."*
Excuse #10: *"I can't do it alone."*

Whatever your particular challenge may be, if you can identify with the challenge of knowing what to do, but you are still not doing it, then I've got life-changing news for you.

These typical excuses can effectively paralyze you — making it virtually impossible for you to take the actions needed to create the change you know you need to, to exit your business on your terms, on your timeline.

In other words, even if you're highly motivated, even if you want something very badly, and even if you know exactly what you need to do to get it; you've set up barriers and you AREN'T going to be able to do it alone.

You can overcome every excuse and every barrier to get to where you want to be at the end of the year. You know where you are and you know where you want to go to make the next 2-5 years your best years yet. Make it happen, and break through every excuse, every justification going through your head so you can get out with the financial freedom for your reinvention.

Can You Answer 5 Questions about Your Exit Strategy

Most business owners will see the title of this book and skip the whole thing. After all, they're too young and too busy in the business. Why should they start planning their exit strategy now?

You're not one of them. That means your eyes have been opened to the imperative of thinking about your exit from the outset – or at least from today forward.

You realize that you have no intention of working this hard for another 5, 10 or 20 years. You've built a business you are proud of, that rewards you nicely today and you want to be able to walk away on your terms on your timeline.

Sounds simple and reasonable. But for many logistical, emotional, and financial reasons, it can't happen overnight. Unfortunately, most business owners neglect the topic, don't consider the decisions, and leave the process to the last moment. Unlike their decisive leadership that got them to this point, they've sidestepped the following questions for various reasons. You don't have to.

Here are five key questions you do want to spend time considering, and exploring the tradeoffs of different answers. Sometimes the answer to one, dictates the answer to others, but if that one answer changes, you open up other latent possibilities you'd never thought of before. When you lay out your answers to these questions, you will be in a better position to take timely steps and integrate all the necessary elements for your exit. You will be in control of effectively negotiating a successful business transaction to achieve your optimum exit.

1. **How much longer do you want to be actively involved in the business?**

Vague answers like 'at least 5 more years' are a way to avoid the question. Dig deeper. Maybe it's easier to look at what you want to accomplish in the business before you're ready to walk away. This date is important because it triggers every other action, trigger and date along the way to get there.

Most successful exit transactions take long-term strategic planning. They can't and don't come together in 60 days. You must start the process before you ever thought it would be necessary because it takes far more time than you imagined to line up all facets to suit you.

To maximize the value of your business when you do exit, you need to have a clear goal for the company and for your own/your family's future.

2. **Who will be your likely successor?**

Have you thought about who should be your successor? Should it be your children, one of your children? Should it be your employees? Or would you look for a buyer well-suited to the business, who can take it to new heights? Maybe you think it's in your customers and staff's best interest to be acquired by an industry giant or your biggest competitor.

There are many options. What's optimal depends on you, your goals, your industry, your company culture.

3. **What do you need out of your business in a transaction or transition, to have the financial independence for your next venture/adventure/ retirement?**

This is really two questions and to answer the first half, you need to answer the second half first.

What will you do next? Do you have a plan? Do you have a project, venture, hobby in mind? Will you travel for two years and then build a house up in the mountains? Will you go back to school as a student or professor? Will you volunteer?

Your plans for your next steps or avocation create the baseline of your financial requirements from any transition or transaction you decide on. Think through your aspirations for the lifestyle you want and the goals on your bucket list that you want to fulfill once you exit this business. Clarify what you'll be doing and what it will take to fund your financial independence. That will set some parameters on your company valuation and the structure of your exit to ensure your future.

Run the numbers so you know how much you need from the deal so you know with relative certainty that you can pursue and achieve your life's goals. That has to include basic living expenses, health care costs, long term care costs; and any education funding for children or grandchildren, travel costs, replacement vehicles, vacation home, weddings, philanthropy, legacy planning, or tax liabilities.

4. **Do you know what your business is really worth on the market?**

You need two numbers. In the end it's up to you to make sure they match.

You need to know how much cash you need to take away from the sale of your business, regardless of the form the transaction takes. And you need to know with brutal honesty the market value of your business – what it is actually worth, not what you think it's worth.

Market value always trumps what you 'need' out of the business. Don't get trapped into terms you don't like because you were only looking at the valuation number. Use independent experts to value the business before you get locked in during a negotiation. They can often show you some strategic changes to increase market value in your favor.

5. **What should you be doing now to minimize your future tax liabilities?**

   Don't look at taxation in isolation. Revisit your business plan now and consider the tax implications for your growth curve. Expand your strategic planning to include contingency planning, succession planning, transition planning, and then run some financial models to see which options look most attractive for your future.

Whether you intend to sell your business in the next three years, or you've set a date three decades from now, it's never too early to start the planning process. Planning now will help you clarify your ultimate goals you are aiming for. Your business will likely be the primary vehicle or source of funding to provide financial freedom so you can achieve every goal you set for the rest of your life and beyond.

PART I
Readiness

CEO Exit Readiness Assessment

Here is a starting point for exploring and considering when and how you might exit/sell your business. This short set of questions will highlight your current thinking, decisions, issues and options.

1. Is your business ready to be sold?
2. Are you ready to get out, leave the business and move on to your reinvention?
3. Who will buy your business – and what form will the transaction take: trade, cash, management buyout, private equity, VC, Employee buyout?
4. What sort of seller will you be?
5. Do you have the right team in place (staff and management)?
6. Do you have the right set of expert advisors on your team?
7. Do you know what it is that you don't know? How do you know that you don't know?
8. Have you already planned your reinvention after you exit your business?

Answer these questions first, before you proceed. Document your answers. Keep track of how your answers evolve and who on your team is aware of these changes along the way.

Top Dollar Strategies

To sell your business for top dollar, be diligent applying these three strategies:

1. **Prevent Seller Neglect** – Just because you've decided to sell, doesn't mean you can neglect the business. You must do everything you can to increase sales, momentum, and customer loyalty right through the exit process until the transaction is done.

   You must keep your eye on current and forecasted sales. Your buyer will pay more for the business with proven increasing sales and forecasted accelerated growth than for declining or stagnant sales with nothing new in the pipeline.

2. **Remove yourself from day-to-day operations** of the business. You need the buyer to see that the value of the business he's buying is in the business, not in you. To maximize the value of the business, you must demonstrate the business can be self-sustaining without your daily presence. They need to see customers, your team, your vendors engage and commit to do business with your company because of the business, not you.

   To do that, train your management team to take on all your responsibilities (not cold turkey but over time). Build the infrastructure to support them to do everything you've always done. The more systems, structure, processes and procedures you have, the more valuable the business. You can monetize every operational task and responsibility that you delegate and transfer to your team.

3. **Reduce the personal rewards and benefits** you take from the business. There are many ways that small business owners can have the business pay for conveniences and luxuries. However, when it comes time to sell your business, buyers will be willing to pay well for your profits. So if you are taking money out of the business for personal expenses (legally), you are reducing profits. That's not appealing to them. When it's time to sell, separate your personal and business expenses. Stop using the business to bankroll family dinners, vacations, cars, country club memberships.

Plan Your Business Exit BEFORE You Plan Your Market Entry

Most traders never plan or even discuss their Forex exit strategy.

In the world of Forex trading, that's what <u>Pete Visconti says</u>. In his world, traders pay more attention to their entry, setting up a good trade and timing profits. They forget or don't look at the cost of not having a Forex exit strategy for each trade too.

As Visconti learned the hard way himself:

Although, traders will argue which is more important,
you need to understand that they both are.
Just make sure they are planned and part of your trade plan.

Analogous to his advice for traders to have a Forex Exit Strategy, here are my four points for Entrepreneurs and CEOs to plan your business exit strategy before you start:

1. **Know What Your Business Exit Strategy Will Be BEFORE You Launch Your Business.**

   If you are in business and didn't do this up front, you are already behind. It's already harder for you to make good clear decisions about your business day to day, because you don't know what your exit options are; what you are aiming for.

   Therefore, if you don't have an exit strategy in place, put exit planning on your critical path now to increase the value of your business at exit – whenever that may be.

2. Consider Multiple Exit Strategies

When you lock down your exit strategy too soon, you eliminate the possibility of alternative opportunities providing even better solutions. When you maximize the number and variety of options on the table; you have more choices, more opportunities, and can make better decisions along the way.

The sooner you start exploring alternatives open to you, the more control and more choices you can position you and your business to benefit from. The longer you wait and the smaller your exit window, the fewer options you can consider and reducing the value you can realize at closing.

3. Always Initiate a 'Stop Loss' as Part of Your Exit Strategy

In the context of your exit strategy, a 'Stop-Loss' is a contingency plan if things go awry and you must get out fast.

You have an emergency exit from the building. You have a backup of your hard drive offsite. You have an emergency call list in case of a blizzard or hurricane. You also need a plan for other crisis scenarios.

It could be an insurance policy, a backup successor, a backup exit plan that is not ideal, but fulfills many of your criteria and can be invoked quickly. It's like having a co-signer on a key bank account or having a second key holder for your lockbox.

4. Stick to Your Exit Strategy just as Conscientiously as You Stick To Your Business Strategy

One of the biggest obstacles business owners face is getting distracted by the 'new shiny object'. They get restless or bored working the sound strategy they are implementing and decide to shake things up without any stopgaps to protect them or the business. That lack of discipline can cost you your retirement and the business in the end. Revise it strategically if necessary. It's in your best interest to trust your exit strategy and follow it with discipline.

Most entrepreneurs will skip these elements of laying out their business. Most CEOs will trivialize the importance of their exit plan in building the success of the business.

The flaw in that thinking is that business is all about making a profit.

Planning your business exit strategy from the outset is an imperative to achieve your goals for the business. Consequently, your daily decisions all lead to how much profit you achieve and what you want to do with the resulting profits.

Inkling to Exit Your Business?

RBS Citizens and Forbes Insights recently produced a new survey entitled *Middle Market M&A Outlook 2012*. http://images.forbes.com/forbesinsights/StudyPDFs/RBSC MiddleMarket M&A2012.pdf . They surveyed the buyer market for M&A (Mergers & Acquisitions) activity. If you are the CEO of a growing business with even an inkling to exit your business in the near future, take note of these findings.

Their insights and commentary are equally useful to exiting CEOs as prospective sellers into this market.

Combining a survey of 432 senior executives with 11 in-depth interviews from companies that ranged from $5-500M in size (45% under $25m); they found that: "most mid-size companies said they had ample cash, while two-thirds viewed today's conditions as a "buyer's market." To this, add the fact that asset prices are at or near historical lows."

Consider each of these Key Findings and how they apply to your situation:

- **Key signals indicate that markets could be ripe for M&A.** Two out of three middle market executives view conditions today as a buyer's market. Meanwhile, two-thirds of the survey respondents also said that balance sheet cash was plentiful—with over a third indicating that they could acquire assets of $2 million or more without incurring debt or injecting equity.

- **Other signals are mixed.** Deal volume is often driven by market participants (aka buyers)' view of future asset values. Only about a third of executives said they believed prices would be higher one year later. However, among the most active acquirers in the survey sample, that expectation rose to one-half.

- **For now, organic growth is the preferred path.** More of today's mid-size companies are focusing on achieving growth through wholly internal means than by any of the corporate development approaches involving mergers, acquisitions, partnerships, or other close collaboration with external counterparties.

- **But companies are very much open to M&A.** M&A is recognized as a source of potentially significant growth. Half of all executives described themselves as active in

M&A, with one out of eight describing themselves as very active.

- **There will be deals.** One in three executives said they were likely or very likely to acquire one or more significant assets over the course of the next year.

- **Most express a merely opportunistic approach.** About one in four executives described their current orientation toward transaction markets as proactive. Their companies are poring over balance sheets and income statements, looking for viable external targets or even potential internal divestitures. Well over half said [that] though not actively seeking a transaction, [they] would be willing to act should a compelling proposition arise.

- **Synergy, though challenging to achieve, still drives valuations.** Synergy, the idea that one plus one can equal an amount greater than two, can be triggered, within a deal premise. Synergies come in two basic forms: cost and revenue. While both can be difficult to achieve, and both are often overestimated; it is revenues that sophisticated acquirers say should be treated with particular skepticism. Two out of three executives said that synergies were a vital component of valuation.

- **Executives perceive a range of integration challenges.** One reason that executives tend to prefer organic growth is that bringing an acquisition online requires considerable focus and resources. Survey participants noted that a number of areas are, at best, difficult to integrate. The areas of greatest concern include IT, sales and marketing, product development, and manufacturing.

- **Deal practitioners are using a wide range of tools.** In performing valuations, executives use multiple lenses. Tools include everything from discounted cash flow models to comparisons of comparable transactions, public company valuations, payback periods, and even real option and multi-variable simulations.

- **Consultants matter.** Faced with the challenges of assessing opportunities, performing valuation, or financing a deal, executives recognized the need for a mix of both in-house and external resources. For those companies most active in the market; valuation, financing, and due diligence are the areas where specialists are most often tapped.

- **We're not for sale.** Three out of five executives bluntly stated their companies were not for sale. Still, the remaining two out of five said they were willing to entertain the idea of being acquired. Only a tiny fraction of survey participants described themselves as anxious. And a note to any would-be sellers: the vast majority of executives viewed carve-out financial statements as at least somewhat or very important. Or put another way, the preparation of reliable carve-out statements can help to ensure a quicker transaction.

Reread these key findings in the context of your business and you being the seller who is being targeted. How can you use these insights to strengthen your own company's position?

Why You Need An Exit Strategy

Business owners do not plan to fail.
But 95% fail to plan. Don't be one of them.

Your business exit is not a death sentence. It should be the ticket to your next venture, adventure, avocation or simply the joy and fun of retirement. Here are just five reasons you need an exit strategy.

1. **Plan B** – Every business owner needs a Plan B. You always have options and contingencies in mind for business decisions and opportunities to consider. When it comes to what you do 'next' after this business, you need options too. Plan B could be as simple as closing up shop and walking away when you get tired of the business. Plan B could be what you'll do next when your hands, your eyes or your legs won't let you do any more of what you've been doing for the last 20 or 30 years. Plan B could be the fulfillment of every promise you made and every dream you've had over the last few decades. If you don't have Plan B, you are in denial.

2. **Plan Ahead** – Every CEO is busy in their business, keeping it going, growing, and thriving. CEOs care about their customers, clients, staff as well as their outside support team, investors and others. But when you stay focused on today, tactics, and to-do's, then your view of the world is narrow and shortsighted. As the CEO, it's your job, nobody else's, to look at the long-term goals and direction of the company, the future of the company and the security of your team. The CEO has the strategic responsibility to plan ahead. Own it and everyone will

benefit. Ignore it or deny it, and your business will drift with no rudder. When you acknowledge your mortality and plan ahead for your exit, you ensure both your legacy and your dynasty will carry on.

3. **Contingencies** – There are business contingencies and there are owner/leader contingencies. As the CEO, you need both in place. Emergencies happen. We have no control over the weather, fire, flood, or earthquake. How will your business continue in spite of/around outside disasters? You need contingencies built in for the short-term or long-term loss of a key team member – do you and your staff know what to do in case someone breaks a leg or quits for health reasons? You need to document a process and a plan for how to proceed so the business doesn't miss a step. Most importantly, do you have contingencies in place so that if you must get out of the business, the business can continue? Have you made you irrelevant to day-to-day operations? These contingency plans reduce risk and add value to the business. They provide the terms and parameters for how you can indeed exit the business while preserving your legacy and dynasty.

4. **Security** – Your business is likely our most valuable asset – and yet it's also probably the most illiquid asset you own. Therefore, while you are working, drawing a paycheck from the business, it is providing security. But as soon as you can't or choose not to continue in the role of CEO, what does that do to your financial security, especially long-term. You need to start building your exit strategy now so this business you've invested so much blood, sweat and tears into will indeed provide for the security of financial independence which you need when

you exit. Setting up and implementing this one element can take years.

5. **Build Wealth** – The biggest mistakes almost all CEOs make in both large and very small businesses, is that they settle into building a business that provides only an income stream. They never set up the business to be a wealth-producing machine. They get to the point where they want to exit and there's nothing there that can be monetized anywhere near the value they think it's worth. Their wealth is so tied into the business; they can't leave with the financial independence they dreamed of.

There is a solution:

With an exit strategy in mind all along the way, then every day-to-day decision is tied to the strategic long-term goal of a specific exit strategy. When you focus on a wealth-producing strategy, the income stream will be there.

You Must Have a Business Exit Strategy

I repeat, *you must have a business exit strategy*. How can I emphasize this enough?

Without an exit strategy, you may get stuck in a quagmire – where you can't get out of your business. Why would you intentionally allow yourself to get into that predicament?

At its worst, an exit strategy will help you save face instead of closing the doors and walking away with nothing. At its best, your chosen exit strategy will tie your transition to the achievement of a specific objective worth more to you than the cost of continuing on as CEO.

When you do decide it's time to move on and you want to 'cash in' on the successful prosperous business you've worked years to build, here are few steps you can take immediately to get started on your exit strategy:

1. There is tremendous pressure associated with every step in the sale of a business. Make time to work on the strategic side instead of focusing exclusively on the tactical/operational side.

2. To prepare for the sale, start thinking about it early: ideally 2-5 years before you intend to walk away.

3. Put yourself in the buyers' shoes. Recognize what they want, what they need, what they'll ask for and what they're looking for.

4. Don't even consider doing this alone. Loners can tell you the <u>best stories about their failures </u>but you don't need to be one of them. Instead, assemble an integrated team of professionals. An exit strategist can become the virtual partner who facilitates your team of licensed experts to produce a cohesive exit solution.

5. Make sure your financials are 'clean' and your projections are sound. You want everything in order well before the sale date.

6. Prepare the business before you get a professional valuation to enhance the value of the business. This will strengthen your negotiating position with prospective buyers. The analogy is that to sell a home you de-clutter and make it spotless to get the best price, which takes time. The same is true, even more so, for your business.

7. Get educated on the process of 'selling a business'. There are many elements, many options, and many players. You want to be in control of the process.

Many CEOs believe the mythology that they can make the decision and exit the business less than 6 months later. In practicality, it takes 2-5 years for an owner to fully exit their business.

Avoidable Risks and Consequences

If you try to rush it, you face many risks and consequences that are avoidable:

1. You reduce your choices

2. You eliminate strategic options to grow (top line, bottom line, etc.)

3. You minimize the value you can get

4. You don't have enough time to think through the integration of personal, professional and business goals

5. You may not be satisfied with hastily chosen results

6. You may not prepare staff and successors enough for an optimal transfer and transition

7. You may not be able to prepare adequately for the tax consequences of your decisions

8. You may not be happy with the outcome even if it is on your accelerated timeline

Tame your exit strategy. Start early. Plan ahead.

Why Are Exit Strategies So Difficult?

Working in a vacuum, the assumption is that exit strategies are difficult.

Most owners assume exit strategies are difficult. That assumption discourages anyone who is considering an exit from getting started early.

As the owner of your growing enterprise, it's easy to be so consumed with the day-to-day operations of the business, that you never find time to think about your exit strategy (*knowing* it is going to be difficult). So naturally, it simply gets shuffled to the bottom of your TODO list and never rises to the critical path until it's too late.

You can minimize how difficult your exit is by being proactive, starting early and committing to the bigger plan to achieve your ultimate goal. As a discerning entrepreneur, you know your business is your largest asset that you need to monetize if you are going to secure your reinvention (not retirement).

Exit planning requires numerous conversations and then an integration of solutions in all the following areas:

- Peak performance
- Succession planning
- Contingency and continuity planning for management and leadership transition
- Business valuation strategies to make the business buyer attractive and buyer ready
- Transition planning to your reinvention (not retirement)
- Tax planning for both the business and the owner
- Estate planning goals and options from wealth advisors and insurance advisors
- Deal structure options both legally and financially

Your exit strategy will be specific to you, your business, your timeline and your goals.

- There is no 'cookie-cutter' approach.
- It doesn't happen overnight.

The difficulty in exit strategies comes from the multitude of possibilities and re-combinations you have to explore and choose from.

You Can't Go To School to Learn This Stuff

Schools just don't teach this stuff, especially for private businesses. They focus on starting and running a strong profitable business, not how you'll get out or how you'll get your money out.

Most business owners only go through the exit experience once in a lifetime. They have no experience or hindsight to draw from to do this right.

There is only limited primary reference material available to teach owners how to plan and manage the business exit. The anecdotal lessons from owners' personal exits reinforce the difficulties of exiting on your terms and on your timeline.

Comprehensive early exit strategy support is in short supply. Effectively executing your exit strategy requires collaborative teamwork from and with your expert advisors. You need to own the exit process as your top priority. An exit strategist can become your most trusted strategic advisor to achieve that end.

An entrepreneur who tries to continue running the company operationally and prepare the company for their most profitable exit, will do neither well. Build an expert team, to indeed plan your exit to achieve your ultimate goal.

Set Your Exit Strategy From the Beginning

Begin With The End In Mind ~ Stephen Covey

There's a lot to consider when you are starting a business. You need to be clear on your mission and vision, your business model, your market research, marketing and sales strategy; and your budget and operations to implement that business plan. It's easy to get busy working in the business, making it a viable concern. That's the fun and the immediate reward for your vision and effort.

However, there's another critical piece that's easy to put off but critical to your long term goals. That's your exit strategy. If you set your exit strategy as part of your initial goal setting then all your milestones and goal achievements will lead towards your ideal exit strategy. Here are six areas to explore to be sure you achieve your end goals.

Is Maximum Value One Of Your Goals?

- What does that mean to you?
- Goal achievement is only possible if you have a goal you want to get to.
  Do you have a number you want the business to be worth?
- How long will it take to achieve your goal, achieve that number?
- How important is that number to your personal long term plans?
- Do you have a number that you need in the bank in order to secure your retirement?

- Do you want to live your legacy and leave a dynasty or do you want to work yourself into an early grave?
- Do you want to pass on the business to family or successors and create an exit package?

These are easy questions to ask. They are hard to answer. If you find yourself not doing this homework or you keep justifying why you don't need to do this now, or you think it doesn't apply to your business, then you are unconsciously jeopardizing your business and your personal future.

Exit Planning Financial Snapshot

There are many aspects to exit planning that business owners take for granted, never think about, or abdicate to others. This naiveté is one of the biggest roadblocks to getting out on terms that give you the full value of the business. The scope of this book is broader, more all-encompassing than just the finances of the exit transaction. You can find many experts and financial models to help with the exit transaction in financial terms and you will need them. You can find a few tools to get you started on my website: www.thiswayoutgroup.com.

To tame the numbers beast before you get there and to make it absolutely manageable for any business owner, here are five core elements to consider on the financial side of exit planning:

1. **Setting Financial Goals**
   Clearly decide and define your long-term income needs and the financial requirements of your reinvention (new venture, avocation, adventure, hobby). What outside income sources will help you meet those income goals? Do you have annuities, trusts, retirement accounts in place? Subtract those values from your long-term income needs. The balance is what you need from your business.

Based on these needs, you can determine the sale price and terms you want your business to deliver when you exit. Initially, these two numbers may not match up. That's just one good reason to start planning early.

2. **Current Value of the Business**

   To be buyer ready, you should always know the current value of your business. You won't be disappointed by a buyer's offer if you know the current fair market value of your business. Valuation experts analyze the business books and other materials and compare its profits and losses to relevant businesses in your region and/or industry. With the current competitive value in mind, you can track your timeline to exit on your terms to meet your financial goals.

3. **Build Business Value**

   To exit early and maximize the value you walk away with, it is imperative to always be building business value. If you are always adding value, accelerating growth and making the business more buyer attractive, you will have the opportunity to exit with the financial freedom for your reinvention. If you have not been building value all along, start now so that you can sell the business for what you know it's worth and meet your long-term financial goals.

4. **Selling a Business**

   Selling a business has many parallels to selling a house. Once you decide to sell and the business is buyer ready, it can still take 6 months to 2 years to close a transaction. Before you absolutely must sell (for any reason), consider all your exit options, all possible buyers and the impact of each option on your exit, on the future of the business and the future employment of your team with the

31

business. Before you choose a specific option, also investigate the tax impact on you and the business. The tradeoffs can be severe.

5. **Life and Legacy Beyond Business**

   With your comprehensive business exit plan and strategic contingency plan in place, you can explore and consider options for reinvention alongside your estate planning goals to leave a legacy and secure your dynasty. Much of your financial independence beyond the business as well as your estate planning are tied to the sale of the business (aka a liquidity event).

You have more estate planning options, more tax advantaged options and more ways to maintain the owner benefits you enjoy; if you start this planning early - ideally, five years before you can fund those options at your exit.

Your financial position, holdings, and control over the business and those holdings, will change drastically and instantly once you sell the business. Therefore, you must revisit your personal financial plan and your estate plan at each business milestone of the exit process. As you make choices for exit options and reinvention opportunities you want to pursue, be sure to circle round to be sure they still coincide with your business exit, continuity and contingency plans.

Stating the obvious, this is not a complete discussion of the financial aspects of exiting your business. It does however give you a general outline of the scope of the financial issues to address with various key experts on your team. Just on the financial side, you can begin to see the value of starting now, planning early and preparation to maximize the value of your business when you want to get out.

What Is Your Timeline To Exit?

Do you have a timeline to achieve your goal? You have a choice starting today.

- You can sell quick, or any time you want
  OR
- You can take the time to position your business to sell high

You can't do both.

I strongly recommend you work actively on your exit strategy **starting now** if you intend to implement it in the next 36 months. You have 12-24 months of work to do before you engage a broker, attorney, or CPA if you want to position your business for optimum sale.

Think about how much work is involved in getting your house ready to sell, improvements, repairs, decluttering, staging and curb appeal. The same is true for your business to get the highest valuation and an ideal buyer.

You need a goal, an exit strategy, a valuation number you are striving for, and a timeline. To do all four, you must do three things:

1. Implement systems for every aspect of your business, in detail.
2. Get the business out of your head and documented.
3. Measure and track your results to produce accurate forecasts.

Align Your Goals With Your Exit Strategy

Do you have goals now? Do you have:

- Daily goals
- Weekly goals
- Monthly goals
- Quarterly goals
- Annual goals
- 3 year goals
- Exit goals

You need all of them if you want to achieve your exit goals. They must be aligned and integrated.

Here's a secret no one talks about but they DO want you to know:

Consistency among all these goals is essential or

- You will fail to exit,
- You will drastically reduce the value, and
- You will pay a premium for the transaction experts in the exit market.

And yet, all of this is 100% avoidable!

The answer is to not just set goals but to stay focused to achieve your goals.

Plan Ahead

You must know your exit date (or at least the criteria for it) and set it at least 2-3 years out – to have time to systematize, streamline and leverage your business to get the maximum valuation.

To get the results you want:

1. Your exit strategy must be part of your initial business plan
2. Your exit strategy must be part of your annual plans every year
3. Your exit strategy must be built into your three year goals from the outset

Where To Start To Increase Value

What can you do to maximize the value in your business? Among other things, to achieve your goal, you must:

Sell more

Increase prices

Reach new markets

Reduce costs

Hire/Train

Document your expertise

Document all systems and procedures

Protect Intellectual Property

Research and prove your market position

Revisit your business plan, vision and mission statements

Clean up customer files

Clean up your financials

Update corporate records

Identify 1-4 was you can increase business value in each of these areas. The cumulative impact will dramatically reshape the value you can command when you want to cash out.

Is The Value Right Now In You Or In Your Business?

Do you know where the value is in your business right now? Is the value in you, the owner/entrepreneur? Or is the value truly in the business itself?

This is the uncomfortable wakeup call for most business owners. Are the expertise and the business strategy all in your head, and in your proprietary files? Are you the only one who understands how the financial books are set up? Here's the risk:

You have nothing to sell and
you have no exit options
if this is still true.

Instead, you can and should start now to:

1. Train others on different pieces,
2. Outsource different pieces, or
3. Start delegating more and more.

Start now because it takes time to transfer knowledge, expertise, systems and processes, never mind responsibilities, to others. In some cases, you'll know exactly what to delegate and who should be doing tasks instead of you. Sometimes you already know who should take on responsibilities or who is ready to step up to take on more responsibility. When you start early, you can train and groom people to grow into positions and responsibility - which ties them to the business more. Both add value to the business when you want to get out.

When you outsource, you have the flexibility to divide up work piecemeal and try different vendors and sources to get work done. When you start early, you can find those vendors who fit your needs and adapt well to suit your corporate culture and become an extension of your team, again adding value. And if a vendor is not an asset when you are trying to maximize value for a potential buyer, you have time to find and train the replacement within your timeline.

When you offload operational responsibilities, you can focus on leadership and strategy to make the business more valuable now and for a future buyer.

The side benefit of delegating, outsourcing and automating is that you free up time to work on your most valuable activities including your exit strategy to achieve your ultimate goal.

Where to Start Before You Set Exit Objectives

Whether you address it from the outset of your business or later down the road, every business owner needs an exit plan. Some business owners intend to sell the business for maximum profit, some want to sell it to successors or employees, others want to go public, and still others intend to keep it in the family.

In each case, taking the time to prepare the exit plan now will allow you, the owner to reach your ultimate goal with a comprehensive 360 view with all the pieces in place. Business-owner exit planning should begin five to 10 years before you want to retire or pass your business to your chosen successors.

Unfortunately, 95% of all business owners NEVER do exit planning. And they wonder why they end up with nothing when, on the day they get fed up and want to sell it as fast as they can; they accept the first offer they receive at less than what their business could be worth.

That doesn't have to be you.

Plenty of expert advisors will tell you that exit planning starts with your exit objectives and the retirement income you want to have – because that's where they start working with clients.

There are a few other pieces you need to define BEFORE you can answer those two questions. They are core pieces of having a strong business foundation long before you consider implementing any exit strategy.

Before you can define your exit objectives, you must identify:

1. Your long-term ultimate goals for the business – with you or without you
2. How you want to secure your legacy now, before you leave

3. How you want to ensure your dynasty once you exit the business
4. Who you want to take leadership of your business (as owner, non-owner manager, or transition staff)

Determine and document what still needs to be done in terms of business planning, contingency planning, and succession planning to position the business for maximum growth and value? Work on that planning first, as a prerequisite to detailed exit planning.

Multiple Objectives

You may have multiple exit objectives. Be sure they are consistent. Then prioritize the outcomes. Selling fast, selling for maximum value and selling for 100% cash up front can be conflicting goals.

As part of your transition planning process, when you define what your next step will be after you exit, you'll get a better idea of how much funding you need: for a new venture, to invest or for philanthropy; not just your personal retirement income. You'll also get clear on your goal timeline and your options for what format the transaction can take.

The lifestyle you intend to pursue after the exit may expand or restrict the exit options you consider.

You don't have to have a plan today.
You do have to start planning today.

The more lead time you invest in building a strong business to achieve your ultimate goals, the more fruitful and fulfilling will be the exit strategy you can choose to implement.

How to Set Goals That Ensure a Successful Exit Strategy

There's a lot on your plate when you start a business. Of course, you need to be clear on your mission and vision, your business model, your market research, marketing and sales strategy and your operations to implement your business plan. As a result, you can be consumed by day to day responsibilities and urgent demands. All of this eats up time.

As I said earlier, there's another critical piece that's easy to put off but very critical to achieving your long term goals. That is your exit strategy.

If you set your exit strategy as part of your initial goal setting then all your goal achievements will lead towards your ideal long-term exit strategy. Here are a few more recommendations to ensure you set goals that get you to a successful exit.

1. **Choose the right exit strategy for your goals**
   You have monthly and annual goals for your business. Commit to your short-term and intermediate goals only if they are aligned with your long term goals and the ultimate goal achievement of your ideal exit.

2. **Set growth goals aligned with your exit strategy**
   Your growth goals are essential to the healthy, strength and survival of your business. When you look at your growth goals, be sure they are taking you in the direction of your exit strategy. Growth that is in conflict with your exit plan or competes with your long term goals will hurt the business and limit your ability to achieve your exit strategy.

3. **Identify goals to increase value**
   The value of the business is not just in terms of assets or cash flow. It's also in your intellectual property which could be in your team, your processes, the relationships

you cultivate and maintain with clients and vendors, etc., not just in your product or brand. So your goals to increase value before your exit could be in these less quantifiable areas that translate into a much higher valuation for the firm.

4. **Plan your exit strategy by intention rather than by default**
   This sounds like a lot of work. In fact, it is. But, if you don't do the work to plan your exit – then your dream of achieving an ideal lifestyle, living your legacy and leaving a dynasty – then you are abdicating both the responsibility and the reward. If you don't plan your exit by design, then you will settle for what you get by default.

5. **Systematize your exit strategy to maximize value**
   The more you can systematize your business so someone else can run it equally well without you, the more a buyer will be willing to pay you to keep it going. The better you are at systematizing everything, the easier it is for a broker to pitch and leverage that value for a higher price. This step takes discipline and consistency starting long before you intend to exit.

Apply these five recommendations to get the results you want. That's how you achieve every goal you set. That's how you ensure your own successful exit strategy.

Goal Achievers Set Goals To Ensure A Successful Exit Strategy. Do You?

Goal achievers begin with the end in mind and an absolute conviction and commitment to achieve their big bold audacious goals. If you have an exit strategy for your business, you are already setting your business up for success, achieving outrageous goals and on track to realize your exit strategy. If you don't have an exit strategy, you are not alone. Most businesses (of all sizes) never plan their exit strategy.

That's not to say this is a good thing; just that the majority of businesses skip this step and then wonder why they can't get out when they want and the way they want.

When Is The Right Time To Plan Your Exit Strategy?

There is no wrong time to plan your exit, unless you never do it.

The right time is the moment you realize that you don't have one. That could be while you are starting your business; it could be when you launch and go live; it could be part of your annual planning retreat or your long-term planning strategy. The wrong time to plan your exit is the last 12 months before you want to move on.

Is It Ever Too Early To Plan Your Exit?

Never. It's never too early to plan your exit. It's your biggest goal for your business. Achieving the goal of your ideal exit strategy is the ultimate accomplishment for a wealth achieving business owner.

Ideally, your exit strategy should be part of your business plan from the outset, not just for businesses funded by investors. You need an exit plan, even if you never got outside funding. If it wasn't part of your business plan or your strategic plan, add it to your agenda for your next annual planning retreat to ensure that starting this year, you will lay out your exit strategy tied to your operational goals.

Follow these four steps to ensure your successful exit strategy:

1. **Take a holistic approach to planning your exit**. That requires systematizing your whole business: not just finances, and cleaning up the books; but also:

   - Succession
   - Ownership
   - Control
   - Extracting value for you and your family
   - Maximizing value before you exit or sell
   - The structure – what's easiest to sell, or what can be monetized most easily
   - Systems ,strategies, process – get them out of your head
   - Team impact – organizational dynamics, contracts, continuity
   - Client/ sales impact.

2. **Consider and evaluate all the possible exit scenarios** that might work for you and your business, e.g., sell a practice or sell your list; buyout by employees or partners, be acquired, appoint a successor or family member to continue the business, IPO. With each option, explore all the variations that might suit you.

   Remember, your choices are greater the sooner you start planning your exit and the clearer you are on the goal you want to achieve and when.

3. **Include your exit strategy in your annual goal setting and strategic planning session**. Align your short-list of chosen exit strategies with every goal they set so that

each goal achievement moves you closer to your exit every year.

4. **Make your exit strategy one of the criteria of every decision you make**, every goal you set, so every goal you achieve is tied to and focused on that ideal exit strategy. This goes beyond setting SMART goals.

Is Your Goal to Produce Wealth?

Is it really? Ideas, inspiration and insights on goals and goal setting abound. That's a good place to start, but it's not enough to get you to the finish line of achieving your goals on your terms, on your timeline.

Goal achievement starts with good goals, goal setting criteria, a timeline and a process. To harvest the wealth in your business, you need to identify your criteria, and what will keep you focused and accountable to ensure you realize that wealth from your efforts.

Any big hairy audacious goal you set must lead to long-term freedom and satisfaction. In business, that translates to driving your business to achieve those long-term goals that will produce wealth, not just an income. A paycheck and profits are not the same thing. One is immediate; the other is a longer focus and strategy.

What's Your Freedom Number?

Do you know what your freedom number is? Is it a minimum income/year? Is it a net worth of $$$? How much would it take for you to feel you have achieved your goal?

Your freedom number is essential to every decision you make in goal setting and goal achievement. You must know your freedom number to make better decisions and continue to move forward toward your goal.

Each person has a set point for wealth, based on your life experiences. For some people it's all about cash flow. For most of us looking ahead to financial freedom, that freedom number ranges in the $Millions.

Your own definition of financial freedom will be key to your plans to get there. An arbitrary number is not useful. Instead, you need to back into your freedom number. It could include such criteria as:

- Own your home – mortgage-free
- Be completely debt-free
- Assets under management produce an unearned income stream that equals or exceeds your after-tax lifestyle expenses
- Legacy building trusts that preserve principal, minimize taxes or provide perpetual income for families, gifting or other philanthropic purposes
- Insurance policies to provide annuities
- Insurance policies to protect your estate in the case of a disability or long-term illness

Your freedom number is only a starting point, a compass heading for you and your advisors to work towards. Indeed, your freedom number will drive your determination to achieve those goals to produce wealth.

Goal Setting Criteria

Now that you know what you need to aim for, you can set better goals to get to your freedom number. There are two parts to any goal setting. The biggest secret to goal achievement is to be sure you pursue the right goals. Therefore: 1) start by assessing your criteria for each exit goal to validate that you are working towards the right goals. Then 2) think them through to ensure success.

Before you take any action, before you even set your great goals for your exit from the business and beyond; there are four criteria you must establish to put each goal on a sound footing.

1. **Be Invaluable**

   To be invaluable to your business and to your clients, you must always deliver your best. You must always be working on those tasks that make you most valuable to the organization and your clients. So before you launch into an ambitious project or campaign, get clear on what makes you invaluable, what's important and maximizes your worth.

   When you apply this criteria to your exit goals, it means that no one else can ensure your exit on your terms. You can't delegate your strategic role in selling the business to anyone inside the company or to your advisors. You are central to the success of that transaction and to ensuring your ideal life beyond the business.

2. **Your Purpose Must Be Bigger**

   Your purpose for your chosen exit option must be greater than just the 'cash-out' number it brings you. Your purpose could be as transparent as to ensure your family's future, to pay for college, to pay off the mortgage, or walk away with the financial freedom for a secure retirement. Your purpose could be to fund a non-profit, or build a school around what you love. Your purpose could be to eliminate cancer or wipe out malaria from your research. If your purpose is more important to you than the money, it should be so big, it pulls you forward, with no regrets about the business you are leaving.

3. **Your WHY**

   Why is it important to you to work so hard this year, now, towards your exit? Because you are supposed to? Because you need to? Because people count on you? When your WHY is really really BIG, it WILL pull you forward; it will compel you. You can't help but work harder and get more done; you will be more strategic in your decision-making to maximize the value of the business, making the business more buyer ready. Even if you think your WHY is the money – say you really want to walk away with $5M cash - go deeper. Dig for the emotion that drives you. Dig for the need that will fulfill you. Without that deeper personal WHY you want this exit, it's easy to waiver and get distracted by day-to-day operational issues.

4. **Be Passionate**

   The more passionate you are about what you will do and how you will help more people:

   a. It will be easier to let go of the business with something more exciting/enriching/rewarding to move on to;

   b. Your timeline will be clear and laid out;

   c. Buyers will know you are committed to this close, that the deal will go through.

   In your exit, it's not all about the financial transaction. To let go and move on, you must be passionate about your reinvention, what you are moving toward, looking forward to doing/having/experiencing. Be clear on what makes you so passionate about your reinvention before you get to the exit transaction.

Only **after** you know these four criteria, only then can you proceed to your exit plan and take responsibility for what you will do and where you are going. At that point, you can effortlessly lay out a roadmap to achieve the exit goals that pull you to achieve that long-term wealth.

With your specific criteria in mind, the right exit goals are:

1. **Measurable**

   Every goal must be quantifiable. If you can't measure it, it can't be a goal.

2. **Achievable**

   To maximize the value of the business to make it more appealing for buyers, you want to show numbers, forecasts and momentum. To help your sales team achieve new heights at the same time as you are taking a less active operational role, break down each goal into increments of the larger goal. Focus on achieving 10% of the new bigger goals. Then achieve it 10 times over. It's easy to repeat what you've already done. The accumulation of these smaller goals will build momentum and confidence to surpass the original goal because all action is aligned with achieving the smaller goal.

3. **Relevant**

   Use relevant numbers. In e-commerce for example, which will drive revenues more: your search engine rank or the click-throughs to the sales page? The answer depends on your business. Focus on what is relevant to your business. Relevance also ensures the exit goal is tied to your purpose and values from your criteria above. Be sure the Key Performance Indicators (KPI) you use are meaningful to potential buyers, not just you.

4. **'Rathole-resistant'**

   [Guy Kawasaki's term] This is the checks and balances piece. Make sure each of your exit goals enhances all the factors that will make your business/organization a viable option for buyers. If you have a goal of monetizing the revenue potential in a new target market as part of your exit price, but you can't prove it will generate sales, that's a rathole. Test each goal to be rathole-resistant before you commit to achieve it. It will make your exit smoother and your negotiations stronger.

Focus On Where You Want To Go

Have you ever had to drive home on snowy roads before the plows were out? or on an icy road? It's slippery, right? You don't feel like you're in control.

What's the rule about how to drive out of a skid or a spin in that situation? Focus on where you want to go, not where the car appears to be going.

It's the same with working on your goals to realize your dreams. You have to stay focused on the goals and not get discouraged or distracted.

The biggest danger for any business owner is the allure of the new shiny object. That new shiny object could be a new tool, a new marketing strategy, an affiliate offer, or a new revenue stream. The danger is that by pursuing the new shiny object, you get pulled off your path, off your timeline, away from your exit goals.

Instead, with your exit goals clearly set and your milestones keeping you on track, you are in a position to evaluate each new shiny object more objectively, as it relates to your priorities. By focusing on your goals with tenacity and almost tunnel vision, you can put those new shiny objects on the shelf, on a list, on the backburner, to consider only if they will accelerate your path to turn your business into the wealth-producing machine you deserve.

Be Accountable

Accountability is one of the hardest things for owners and entrepreneurs to commit to. These 8 rules are not new, but they are essential to achieve the goals that will produce the results you desire. Embrace them to achieve your wealth producing exit goals.

1. **Postpone, De-emphasize Or Quantify Less Tangible Goals** such as 'create a great work environment'. Focus on those goals that will create wealth.

2. **Communicate Each Goal** clearly to every single employee/contractor/team member. This is not a one-time task. Communication must be reinforced frequently and consistently. Make sure each person understands how their job relates to the company goals. Encourage feedback to insure everyone understands and is committed to those goals. Track your communications with the team and measure the impact on performance, productivity and profits.

3. **Measure Progress Weekly** If you don't want the accountability of measuring, then you might as well skip the goal setting and a profitable exit too. Measuring monthly is not enough to obtain accurate positive results for you or your team.

4. **Responsibility** Identify a Single Point of Responsibility for each goal. Lousy employees avoid responsibility. Good employees accept responsibility. Great employees seek responsibility. As the leader, which category do you exemplify? The more you can delegate to great employees, the more effectively the organization can operate without your day-to-day presence.

5. **Follow Through On Each Goal** Not every goal will focus on the cool stuff (new software, creative presentation,

etc.). It's not hot or glamorous to balance the budget, resolve all website bugs within 48 hours, or take customer complaints but these tasks are essential to make the business a wealth-producing machine.

6. **Reward Achievers** including you. This sends a message to everyone. Achievers will get reenergized about doing their jobs. Everyone else gets the message that you are building a company that values execution and results, and takes them seriously.

7. **A Culture of Execution** It's not a one shot deal. It's a way of life, part of the corporate culture, the fabric of the company that adds measurable value. To establish a culture of goal execution: set an example by meeting your own operational and strategic goals, empower your employees with the tools, training and support they need to achieve those goals, respond to clients effectively, and measure the progress of each team member.

8. **Morpheus** in The Matrix, gave Neo a choice between the red pill and the blue pill. That cold, brutal reality Morpheus offered Neo is your ally for execution of your goals to achieve your exit move on to your reinvention. Find your Morpheus to distribute the red pills and enable your team to see things as they really are to get optimum results.

Start with your freedom number and only set goals you can focus on and want to be accountable for achieving, to produce the wealth you desire.

PART II
Three Pillars Worldview

Three Pillars

When you decide to exit your business, and walk away from the business you built that you've owned from inception, you need three pillars to your foundation to make a successful exit.

They are your:

- Mindset
- Skill Set
- Knowledge

At Bates College I caught the value of the college motto "*Amore Ac Studio*" [with ardor and devotion] which I internalized as a love of learning. The most successful business owners, who indeed maximize the value of their business, are perpetual students. They are voracious readers, students, and learners.

You choose what you can learn and what you can be taught. Specific to exit planning success, every business owner must become a student of:

- Mindset
- Skill Set
- Knowledge

to successfully sell, scale or install a successor in their business.

What you do with what you learn is key. That takes self-reflection, a "willingness to learn more about their own fundamental nature, purpose and essence".

Mindset

Your mindset going in to exit planning is the most critical determinant of your successful outcome. Your mindset will determine your ability to set and achieve your hopes and dreams. You have to be able to recognize and adhere to the process to achieve them. Most CEOs have dreams and goals of the outcome they want from their business. Many fewer CEOs reverse engineer their goals into a timeline, process, and a sequence to get to that exit.

Challenges will occur that could derail your exit plan, guaranteed. Fighting or resisting those challenges is an unproductive waste of time and energy. Instead, install and master a mindset to address, overcome, resolve, and circumvent each challenge as it arises.

Attitudes and mindset are often ignored or minimized when exploring what we need to learn to achieve our goals and get to an exit.

Most CEOs resist addressing or developing the right-brain skill of mindset readiness which requires the most time to develop and is not easily measured or demonstrated. But your mental and emotional attitudes (your mindset) are the most important of all learning components because that is the gatekeeper that determines how well you acquire, master and apply any other skill set and knowledge.

Entrepreneurs often adhere to tired outdated thinking which in turn sets up their business to continually struggle, to not achieve its full potential, and to settle for selling their business for only a fraction of its worth. That downfall is totally preventable.

What are your attitudes and beliefs? What are your expectations? Which of the following apply to you?

- Have no exit goals
- Have trouble setting exit goals
- Don't know how to set exit goals
- No consensus on exit goals
- Can't delegate/afraid to delegate
- Prisoner of the entrepreneur's trap - Trying to wear all the hats
- Scared to grow – because of past experience, old belief systems, systems or staff that slow or prevent your growth
- Scared to share control, responsibility, ownership or profits
- Scared of losing control
- Easily distracted – by environment, people, events, equipment
- Minimal goals/easy goals/short-term goals that don't stretch individuals or the organization – to play it safe
- No personal accountability of the leadership team/ of you
- Still running the business as an opportunist
- Resist building a strong business foundation for growth or increased value
- Ignore or deny the need for exit planning, contingency planning, continuity planning, succession planning, transition planning, and reinvention planning

You've heard the phrase:

Your attitude determines your altitude.

Your mindset is the key to everything you will achieve to exit your business when you want to. When you decide each of these elements is important enough to the business and to your future beyond the business, only then will you take action and:

- Develop the skill sets
- Acquire the necessary knowledge (direct learning or surround yourself with experts)
- Develop plans, strategies, and tactics to achieve everything you want for your business and from your business when you exit.
- Apply the discipline and leadership to accelerate growth and maximize value on your timeline.

It's a mindset – Your Mindset
You're only limited by your own imagination, determination and ability to see beyond the problems, challenges and roadblocks to all your opportunities.

What Is An Exit Mindset? Why Do I Need It?

Mindset is the most critical of the three pillars, the hardest to develop and it's the pillar you must reset and anchor first.

Your mindset about your exit includes successes, challenges, mistakes, expertise, motivation, confidence, joy, satisfaction about all you have achieved in the business since the beginning when it was a glint in your eye, through the intervening years to the present; as well as what you bring to the exit process over the next two to five years.

Your mindset when you started the business was based on assumptions, enthusiasm, belief, courage and passion. You were invincible and persistent in your devotion and commitment to do whatever it took to make the business thrive. You never let

56

doubts interfere with your goals, ambitions and conviction that you could achieve your most audacious goals. In a young company, your mindset focus is always forward.

Your mindset over the years has settled a bit. You've learned a lot of lessons through survival and growth. You have different assumptions now about business, the market, your clients, even your team, based on years of experience. Your attitude could be as happy and confident as when you first opened your doors but your mindset is based on a wide breadth of experience now, not just enthusiasm. Or, time and experience could have taught you to narrow your focus to what you can control and address today; to focus on the orders coming in and what marketing it will take to increase those orders. Your success mindset as you grow the business expands to include wisdom and insight from past experience to contribute to goals and decisions today. That's where most business owners are flourishing today. The only thought they have of the future is achieving the stretch goals they set for the business for the next 12 months – not 3 years or 5 years, never mind a future any further ahead.

Your success mindset for growing the business, growing the team, adding capacity and building a stronger business foundation probably has nothing to do with when and how you'll exit the business. More than likely you never built an exit plan into your business plan at the outset. Today, entrenched in your success and growth mindset, you don't have time to focus on the future coming closer every day.

. An exit mindset is not the demise of the business; it's a new beginning for you in a new direction and a new beginning for the business under new management.

It's easy to let this slip. We're all more comfortable with old habits than building new ones. It's easier to ship standing orders and keep marketing costs down because the market is still soft.

But those habits conflict with your exit objectives. That conflict first takes hold in your thoughts. When you struggle with cultivating an exit mindset to shift your priorities away from day to day operations and start applying effort and time to the strategic side of the business to prepare it for a new owner – that's when it's easy to sabotage the whole exit plan. That's when you see owners who tell their advisors to get things lined up and seek out potential buyers but can't let go enough to sign the papers.

The exit mindset is a process to work through to ensure you are rewarded for the value you've built up in the business and to prepare you for what's next on your terms and on your timeline.

Exit planning is a whole new job that you never had before and you'll probably never have again. Your exit mindset will decide if this is a rewarding experience leading to the lifestyle of your dreams or a traumatic experience that wears you out even before you close the deal.

Transitioning to and maintaining an exit mindset shifts your priorities, focus and goals. With an exit mindset, any strategic decision you make in the business will be driven by a desire to show growth and add value for the buyer, and maximize the liquidity and financial freedom for your reinvention after the exit.

This mindset shift is taking all the strengths, assets, experience and opportunities for your business and applying them to one specific outcome – your exit on your terms on your timeline.

Exit planning is a completely new job that you never had before and you'll probably never have again. Your exit mindset will decide if this is a rewarding experience leading to the lifestyle

58

of your dreams or a traumatic experience that wears you out even before you close the deal. Everyone exits one way or another, you have a choice.

Transitioning to and maintaining an exit mindset shifts your priorities, focus, and goals. Now, any strategic decision you make in the business will be driven by a desire to show growth and add value for the buyer while maximizing your liquidity and financial freedom for your reinvention after the exit.

This mindset shift takes all the strengths, assets, experience and opportunities for your business and applies them to one specific outcome – your exit on your terms on your timeline. They include all your:

Drive	*Determination*	*Belief - spiritual*
Passion	*Resiliency*	*Conviction-*
Inspiration	*Clarity*	*emotional*
Motivation	*Focus*	

That's a big shift. It's a shift that most business owners do not and cannot make. They get stopped right here in their mindset along with their naïve exit criteria.

Emotional issues that business owners struggle with are a major barrier to planning their exit. They are barriers because they are never explored or addressed. I highlighted this in my report, **Don't Murder Your Business**. Just to touch on the subject here, the emotional issues business owners struggle with have to do with the fear factor. The following are just a few:

- **The fear of letting go**. This has been your baby. Like most owners, you have identified your life through your business. Deservedly so. How do you say goodbye to all of that? What is your identify beyond the business?

- **The fear of loss of wealth**. It took a long time to build the business to what it is today. Once it is gone, you may fear you could lose everything and you need to protect the wealth you built.

- **The fear of loss of control**. This is your business. You built it and no one else can run it as well as you have.

- **The fear of conflict**. Examples:
  1) Two of your kids want to be the next CEO. You don't want to make a choice and then have to deal with family fights.
  2) Your partner doesn't want to retire yet but needs you to stay in the business to make it work for him.
  3) Your partner wants his kids to succeed us but they don't have the financial strength to buy you out.

Emotional issues that you could set aside in launching or growing a business need to be identified and resolved early in the exit process. Those emotional issues could very well be the actual top reason many business owners do not have a written plan for how to get out and never take action to achieve their reinvention. It is human nature to withdraw from and avoid pain. When left unspecified and in doubt, these subjects compound the difficulty and complexity of exiting your business with maximum wealth for your reinvention.

As The CEO, Are You Expendable?

If I were to ask you, the CEO/owner of a thriving enterprise, 'Are you expendable?', what would your answer be? The automatic knee-jerk reaction is 'Of course not. I'm the CEO. I'm indispensable to the organization.'

But, in fact, in business, that's the wrong answer! Indeed, wearing your CEO hat, you want to become expendable. You want to be planning for your exit from the outset, from the very beginning.

To achieve your goal of being an ultra-successful entrepreneur, becoming expendable must be part of your exit strategy.

Your big payday, when you get to cash out on your business, is when you exit (e.g., when someone else buys your business). If you are still indispensable to running the business; if all the intellectual property, goodwill and value of the business is tied up in you; the business is not buyer ready. If the business is not buyer ready, your big payday is still just a hope and a dream.

Once you decide to exit the business, one of your primary tasks is to transition day-to-day operations and transfer that responsibility to your team. To increase the value in the business, to ensure that value can be monetized you, as a successful entrepreneur, must make yourself replaceable therefore expendable.

Failure to shift responsibilities and remove yourself from any operational role is a big mistake that exiting CEOs struggle with. It's emotional, it's strategic, and it's tactical.

Just as you didn't build the company or grow the company overnight, you can't disengage from daily operations overnight. You can't go from being indispensable working long hours, to being expendable overnight. These pieces of your exit strategy take time. They take time to plan and implement – likely years before you exit successfully.

To Get Out of Your Business - Don't Get Emotionally Stuck in Your Business

One of the biggest blind spots for owners is how emotionally attached they are to the business, which can make it very difficult to exit or sell the business.

Owners can and do put on blinders that actually set them up to sabotage or murder their own business. In fact, over 95% of all business owners still do this.

Most CEOs go into business because they are very good at something and/or they love it very much. They put heart and soul and an overabundance of sweat equity into the business they are passionate about. Over time, the business can and often does consume them, their life, and their identity. They become one with the business.

This emersion in the business is essential for the business to survive and become a thriving enterprise. So to an extent, it's very very good, up to a point.

This commitment is essential to building the business, establishing the culture, building out the team to run with and establishing a clear value for the business. But this oneness with the business can cause damage as you start to consider when and how to get out of the business.

You are emotionally stuck in the business when:

1. You can't let go enough to take a vacation, never mind 'retire'.
2. You have no identity, social life, purpose outside of the business.
3. You can't delegate day to day operations because no one can run the business the way you do.

These are just a few of the red flags that indicate you are not prepared to move on, never mind exit the business.

First recognize how you are emotionally attached to the business, then identify why. Then you will be ready to make the changes to reposition your role so you can get out of your business. It takes conscientious, diligent hard work to make the transition to actually get out of your business.

The easiest way to start is with a plan for what's next. Brainstorm on ideas/possibilities/opportunities of what's next for you when you do exit. Do they include a new venture? An adventure (solo or with family)? An avocation, service or hobby? Then explore what has to change in the business to free you up so you can exit and pursue/fulfill these latent possibilities and opportunities.

To exit, you need to get emotionally unstuck from the business and emotionally charged up about your next reinvention.

Skill Sets

Management and leadership skill sets are not the same thing. When you are planning to get out, your technical skills in the business can't be where you focus your time and energy. This is not the time to expand your management skill set either. Rather, your focus must be on leadership and strategy.

In the area of skill sets struggling strategic CEOs lack, do you experience any of these?

- No time to plan
- Can't stick to the plan
- Can't delegate/afraid to delegate
- Stuck in systems and tools that hold you back
- Still using systems and structures you have long outgrown
- Trying to wear all the hats
- No control of financials
- Trying to be the technician and the visionary
- Never enough time for your most important activities
- No time for strategy and planning
- No tracking/monitoring/measuring
- No accountability in the organization
- Poor time management skills
- Mismatch between market needs and company capacity to serve and respond
- Use/misuse/lack of automation or relevant technologies
- Too much operational responsibility to focus on CEO oversight role
- No development of management or grooming of successors

If any of these is a challenge, then you are still working too much in your business. Instead, you need to prioritize working on your business. You need to build up your strategic skill set. These are the core responsibilities you will be responsible for in exit planning.

To take on more strategic responsibilities and help the organization morph into a structure and business model that can grow to fulfill its true potential, you must delegate operational roles, responsibilities, tasks and control. This does not happen overnight. This transition goes hand-in-glove with you exploring your exit goals and exit options.

The Strongest Businesses Around The World
Reach For Big Goals And Achieve Them

Would you like that for your business?

Would You Like To Achieve Every Goal You Set?

You know that goal setting and goal achievement are two different things. Everyone can get to the starting line and set goals for their business if they choose to.

But the latest statistics prove that 95% of all businesses NEVER achieve their goals; business owners never get to exit and are leaving 30-50% of the value of their business on the table. You see only 5% of all business owners ever follow-through to get to the finish line of an exit transaction so they can transition to their reinvention.

I'm not alone in broadcasting these shocking results. According to Jay Abraham there are three reasons for that very low success rate:

1. Entrepreneurs don't start by having any goals, never mind an exit plan. They only have hopes and dreams.
2. They never take action
3. They don't have a step by step plan to achieve their goals, get out, and move on.

Ninety-five percent of all businesses are stuck at a point where the owner takes home enough to pay the bills - $35-40K. They are so busy in the business just meeting their expenses and covering payroll; that they never take time to look at what it would take to make their business into a multi-million dollar enterprise.

For some businesses, it could be as simple as finding ways to increase volume or to increase prices. But for other businesses, it may mean exploring how to leverage strengths, exploring how to expand into new markets or even pursuing new revenue streams or new business models.

Reports at the Exit Planning Exchange Summit 2010 substantiated this lack of planning saying:

75% of the businesses who seek out exit experts (attorneys, brokers, M&A, investment bankers, wealth advisors):

1. Have **no plan** and
2. **Don't know what to do** with the business when they do want to exit.

Settling for where you are because you don't know how to take the next step, or you don't have time to research your options, or you don't have the cash flow to hire the team to achieve your dreams and goals – these are all excuses we feed ourselves.

Remember the campfire story of 'going on a bear hunt' It's told as a round with everyone slapping their knees and pounding their feet to the rhythm. The refrain at each obstacle encountered is a version of:

'Can't go over it, can't go under it, can't go around it, gotta go through it.'

For every challenge and adventure the hunters face, they overcome it and find the bear.

Instead of settling, you need to equip yourself for your bear hunt, to maximize the value of your business so you can transition to your reinvention.

Your exit skill set must include mastery of the following:

- Emotional Intelligence (EQ) skill set
- Leadership
- Time Management
- Productivity
- Planning and Strategy
- Implementation
- Delegation
- Automation

If your goal is to get through the day, meet payroll, go home at night and enjoy the perks of ownership as business deductions, you can continue on with business as usual.

But if you want to accelerate growth, maximize the value and make your business extremely buyer attractive and buyer ready, there are other skill sets you must master starting now. This skill set takes two to five years to learn, evolve, refine, implement and master.

You might say these are soft skills, that these skill sets are not essential to how you run your business now and conclude that they are not necessary. That may be. However, unless you are content to walk away with only 50-70% of the value you know is in your business (the value you are planning on liquidating to fund your reinvention plans); you need to apply each of these skill sets across every department, product line and your entire team.

Consider how each skill set once learned will benefit the business (i.e., add tangible, measurable value to the bottom line) and your exit.

Emotional Intelligence (EQ) IS a Skill Set

Emotional health must be taught and modeled. This is a core leadership skill set. For all of us, emotional intelligence encompasses five basic areas of mastery. They are:

- Knowing your feelings and using them to make life decisions you can live with.
- Being able to manage your emotional life without being hijacked by it; not being paralyzed by depression or worry, or swept away by anger.
- Persisting in the face of setbacks and channeling your impulses in order to pursue your goals.
- Empathetic reading of other people's emotions without their having to tell you what they are feeling – and making time to identify unmet needs.
- Handling feelings in relationships with skill and harmony - being able to articulate the unspoken pulse of a group, for example.

The scope of these skills means there is indeed room for all of us to learn, grow, and improve. There is a lot to learn here. Learning about emotional intelligence, and learning about the tools to develop these skills; that's only the beginning.

It's like reading all the books on sailing and small boat sailing. You then have the theory mastered, but you have no hands-on practice. It's only with practice that we gain mastery of anything. That's true of our feelings and emotions too!

Assessment tools are a great way to learn to identify your emotions. - Energy efficiency tools are invaluable in helping you tap into inner wisdom and resources to manage your emotions and understand what the best choices are when you are making big life decisions.

Persistence can be learned. In fact, providing challenges and hardships to children, to give them an opportunity to develop persistence and stick-to-itiveness, is intrinsic in many cultures. Goal-setting and weekly plans are just two tools you can apply immediately.

Developing empathy is powerful in critical business situations like a client sales call; closing the sale of your business; your management style, etc. Using emotional intelligence tools and skills will allow you to pay attention to your instincts instead of second-guessing yourself.

Once you learn to be the manager of your emotions, it becomes an easy habit to apply in any business or personal relationship.

Mastery of all the basics does not occur overnight. But with practice it comes very quickly - just like learning to ride a bicycle. Once you experience how it's *supposed to work*, how it is *supposed to feel*, it's easier and easier to reestablish in a variety of circumstances. That's where mastery is achieved. That's where you and everyone in your business benefit from your mastery.

This skill set is essential and a critical element for you to successfully navigate the transformation of your business into a wealth producing machine with a championship team the buyer will want to hold on to. Your mastery of emotional intelligence sets the bar for your entire team. If you are stressed out by the exit options or due diligence, your team could run. If you are in control, leading the exit process confidently, your team will do anything to ensure the best outcome.

Your Exit Skill Set Must Include Leadership
When you decide to sell/scale or pass on your business to a successor, you can't abdicate and retire <u>on</u> the job. Your continued leadership is essential to achieve the best result for you, your team and the business. Your exit skill set must include leadership. Your leadership, not management, will attract ideal buyers.

Great leadership is the key to success. Great communication is the key to great leadership. Think of any great leader in modern time: Gandhi, Martin Luther King, Jr., and John F. Kennedy come to mind immediately. They were powerful leaders because they could inspire people to follow them. It was their ability to articulate their vision that made them successful in achieving their goals.

What will it take to transform you from an operational President to a strategic CEO? What will it take to lead your business to conclude the best possible exit to guarantee your reinvention?

In your organization you must be the leader who inspires the team to great heights. To get them to follow you, be sure they are listening to your vision and values (or if needed, include your team in reestablishing them), and then establish the right environment for them to thrive and grow.

Values
When I mention values, everyone nods their heads as if to say 'of course, Kerri, that's obvious'. But, when I check up on this piece, I find the last time they discussed their values - personal and professional-- with their team, was often in the interview before their people were even hired.

You must clearly know your personal values and your organization values to lead effectively. For example, do the answers to these questions come readily to mind?

Personally:

1. What do you stand for?
2. What is most important to you?
3. What would you like your life to demonstrate?
4. What is your personal mission in life?

Professionally:

1. What dos the company stand for?
2. What are you willing to do to get new business/ maximize profits/sell the business?
3. What are you not willing to do?
4. Is there a professional mission statement that is aligned with the actual operation of the company?

Quality leaders don't change their values over time or to achieve short-term success. Consistent core organizational value systems form the strong foundation for long-term success.

A simple definition is that your values are the rules by which you play the game. A well-defined value system makes all decisions easier and encourages your team to go where you lead.

Vision

It's easy to say you have a vision for your business. It's your lifeblood. You know it inside out. Writing it down is the next step. Sharing it widely with your team is imperative too. Even more importantly, your vision for the business must provide a unifying picture so that everyone on the team - regardless of job function - can see exactly where you're taking the business and the importance of their role in getting there. Therefore, the clearer the concept and the clearer (i.e., short and simple) the message is, the more likely you, and your team, can achieve the outcomes you are striving for (e.g., financial, customer relations, growth, market opportunities, product development, etc.) Attention to your vision is crucial to ensure your efforts are always leading towards your desired exit plan

Your vision needs to answer three questions. And it must answer those three questions for everyone on the team.

1. What do we do?
2. How do we do it?
3. For whom do we do it?

As Jim Collins proved in his book, _From Good to Great_, this is not a 30 minute, one meeting exercise. This requires 100% participation. It can't be a top-down decision. It must be iterative and inclusive. You need to test that vision statement in those exact words in the marketplace, with vendors and most importantly with your team.

Your vision and exit plan must agree. Being laser focused on your vision in every area of your business is vital to being able to think strategically. Strategic thinking is the key to achieving every goal you set because it helps you reassess and stay focused on the present opportunities leading to your long-term goal(s).

If you skip this step, it's harder to create that curb appeal to make your business buyer attractive.

You must capture and keep the heart
of the original and supremely able man
before his brain can do its best. - Andrew Carnegie

Environment

When you understand what is at the core of your team members, you can serve them and allow them to reach their full potential. Value their uniqueness. Your team members are your internal customers. You must treat them at least as well as your external customers. This is the highest level of customer service.

Shape the right work environment and you'll have loyal team members to lead. That means, you have to create a work environment that respects each person, appreciates them and rewards their effort, and encourages an openness to change. Make it a safe environment, one which encourages trying new ideas. When you unleash personal creativity, each team member has a stake in the outcome.

It's an environment that promotes growth at all levels. When that environment is part of the corporate culture and value structure that produces accelerated growth, increasing profits and team loyalty, that environment can be monetized. That environment becomes an asset you can monetize and leverage in the valuation of your business.

Combine all three elements, Values, Vision, Environment and you have a leadership formula for inspiring excellence and leading to breakthrough success.

Time Management

In isolation, goal achievement, time management and productivity are immense skill sets to master for yourself and inculcate into your team. Business owners tend to get stuck in silos of focusing on only one skill set at a time. Intention, determination and focus are essential traits to achieve your goals, most especially on the road to your exit.

The way to leverage that time, energy, commitment and focus is to integrate your work. Indeed, there's an alternative to working on your exit goals and getting good at that at the expense of not managing your time or crashing productivity statistics. Integrate all three into systems and processes to eliminate competition.

When you synchronize achieving your exit goals, time management and productivity, a few things can happen:

1. Coordinated control of goals, time and priorities. Goals get clearer and timelines get tighter
2. Easier delegating – assigning and accepting responsibility. The right person is responsible for each task/project, and they are not all you, the CEO.
3. Time management skill sets gets sharper, allowing you and every team member to be more productive. With mastery of time management tools and productivity habits, you will more likely hit your exit milestones on schedule.
4. Hiring and staffing to achieve your growth projections will be based on time and productivity, not guesswork
5. Even as you accelerate growth, you get more time off
6. Fewer detours, dead-ends, delays or do-overs, saving time and money every time. With those processes documented, you can monetize them for your buyers.
7. Productivity systems and habits can free up 25% of your time.

I believe your ultimate goal achievement lies somewhere beyond the business exit itself, fulfilling your bigger purpose, freed of day-to-day management, living the lifestyle of your dreams with much more time off. Time management is one of those critical exit skill sets to master to get it all done.

Productivity

By definition, productivity is a measure of output from a production process, per unit of input or more simply yielding results, benefits or profits. Productivity is distinct from profitability. Profitability is the net difference between revenues and expenses. However, every little improvement to productivity has a direct impact on your profitability.

Until you monetize lost productivity, nothing will change. Take a week to track how you/your team use time. Review and discuss what you find. In discussions with clients, we talk about productivity in terms of the results they need and how to get more done in less time and reduce the cost to do so. You can too, just by being more aware of it.

Here are just three examples of lost productivity:

- Fifteen percent of all paper handled in businesses is lost, *according the Delphi Group, a Boston consultancy*
- **Thirty percent of all employees' time is spent trying to find lost documents.** *Jane M. Von Bergen (Knight Ridder Newspapers), The Boston Globe, 3/21/2006*
- **Executives waste six weeks per year** searching for lost documents.
  From a survey of 2,600 executives by Esselte, maker of Pendaflex and Dymo, FastCompany Magazine, 8/2004

These statistics and others like them are clear evidence that organizations of all sizes desperately need productivity training to take control and get organized.

Consider what the results would be for your business if you were asked about the time you spend on just four activities:

- Email and Internet Use
- Stress and Work/Life Balance
- Time and Multi-tasking
- Paper and Filing

And the dollar cost to your business' productivity for each of these, what would the answer be? How could you increase your productivity in that area? How could you improve productivity in that area for every employee in every department?

When you look at your productivity and the team you have built around your business, can you see inefficiencies in how things get done? What is it costing you to continue to do things the same way? If you monetize that lost productivity, how would you choose to spend those resources? Getting more done? Saving time? Saving money? Increased profitability? Spending more time with friends and family? Taking that vacation?

Demonstrating and documenting productivity improvement efforts directly adds value to your team and adds value to the business itself that your prospective buyer can visibly see in action.

You instinctively know when you are being extremely productive. You get more done. You get more of the right things done. You effortlessly get the most important things done. Isn't that when you are focused on your highest priorities?

Too often we equate productivity with being 'busy', 'very busy', 'too busy'. It is easy to be extremely 'busy' reading all the newsletters in your inbox or filing away all the files and reports you've used all day, but that's not productivity.

Instead, ask yourself:

Is this the most valuable activity I should be doing right now?
What's the most important thing that has to happen today and has
to be done by me?

To get more time and achieve your goals, be sure you do two things: increase productivity in the allotted time, and always address your highest priorities first.

To Increase Productivity

To get more time, and get more done in the time you have, you need to increase productivity. These five new habits will pay dividends.

1. Set your daily task list to address your goals first. Commit to the next step for each goal and get it done first.
2. Set aside a time and place to work uninterrupted (no appointments, no calls, no emails, no distractions).
3. Tackle the most critical task of the day when you are at your peak for performance; often you will be most productive early in the day. In the context of exit essentials, you will ideally work on your exit plan and all aspects of it every day, first thing.
4. Limit the time you expend on reading and answering email, say 30 minutes twice daily – and stick to this rule. Like a diet, you'll see the difference over time, not overnight.
5. Organize your time to group 'like tasks' together. For example, it's more efficient to make all your calls/callbacks at the same time. You're in control, and with a list of calls to make, you can more easily keep each call short and to the point.

Priorities and productivity are co-dependent objectives when you are trying to get something done. Both require focus, discipline, responsibility and accountability.

Focus On Priorities

To say focused on your priorities:

1. Be sure the first task you tackle each day moves you closer to achieving your biggest goals. Your biggest goals should be what helps you cash out when you want to.
2. Delegate what does not have to be done by you.
3. Focus on what's important in order to eliminate crises. Crises take you off your game to address another need on the critical path or on someone else's priority list.
4. Set time limits for every task on your list:
   a. to ensure you complete every task on your list
   b. to stay highly productive using your time wisely on every task you take on.

There's a very compatible synergy between priorities and productivity. Cultivate this kind of inter-dependence and you'll get more done.

Strategy and Planning Add Value to Your Business

You probably built your strategic plan when you launched your business. More than likely, you have not looked at it, never mind used it as a guide for building out your business. When you start preparing for your exit, that strategic plan and any newer versions become valuable intellectual property as well as strategy. Your strategy will be a key selling feature of the business that will attract ideal buyers. It should articulate the goals, objectives and prospects of your business, and the implementation of your vision. Your strategic plan outlines the objectives you will achieve, the order, the timeline and the tactics to be used. Your strategic plan becomes the blueprint for your company's success and your successful exit.

Strategic Planning Benefits

Still not sold on the value of strategic planning in your company?

Some of the purposes of strategic planning include:

- Communicating goals and objectives to all stakeholders
  - team
  - vendors
  - clients
  - shareholders
  - investors
  - experts/advisors
  - prospective buyers
- Identifying Key Performance Indicators to be used to assess and measure progress
- Preparing and providing a mechanism for change [to be invoked when needed].
- Providing focus and direction for all constituents
- Pro-actively solving potential problems in the company before they occur

Resulting benefits include:

- Ensuring the most effective use of company resources
- Ensuring maximum efficiency, effectiveness and integration across all departments
- Increasing productivity by instituting processes, procedures, accountability, tracking and measuring
- Improved communication, team cohesion and recognition of accomplishment as goals are reached.

When To Do Strategic Planning?

When and how long to spend on strategic planning depends on the company itself. At a minimum, any company serious about achieving goals, must allocate time for long-term planning, goal setting and review on a consistent annual basis which should tie every goal, every system, every budget and hiring decision to your exit criteria and timeline. This annual project must be sacrosanct.

Especially, if you are already within the five-year window of your target exit date, there can be no exception, no excuses for not doing strategic planning.

But strategic planning is not just an annual event. You must then roll it back into goals, planning and tracking each quarter, each month and each week. At this granular level, your plan will drive every decision, every expense and every task each employee works on thus increasing productivity and value daily.

Following this plan will help you position your company as one that ideal buyers will be eager to scoop up – maybe even before your target date.

Implementation

The attorneys report that historically, only 10% of all the deals business owners want to implement, get to the closing table and get done. The list of reasons why they fail is lengthy. It comes down to the owner's lack of preparation and stamina in mindset and skill set to get the job done.

An implementation is the realization of an application, or execution of a plan, idea, or policy. A strategic plan and an implementation plan are not the same thing. The strategic plan tells you what to do, why, when and the budget to do it.

The implementation plan spells out the details of how, the resources, timeline, requirements, etc. to fulfill the plan by specified concrete measures Your strategic plan and your implementation plan are two sides of your exit planning to think through thoroughly.

The key to your successful exit is implementation. Full implementation of your desired exit option, to transition to your reinvention, requires following through on a detailed, well-constructed plan. Your exit plan has many moving parts. You must constantly orchestrate all of them. Internally, you must coordinate your team, successors, experts, vendors, clients, budgets, prices. You must align the company goals, market value and corporate objectives with your personal exit criteria and priorities. Executing your exit plan cannot be delegated or outsourced. You must take charge of every step of this implementation to ensure you get to the closing table on your terms, on your timeline.

The challenge to your successful exit is also implementation. It's a big load. Often, most of the pieces need to stay confidential and independent of day-to-day operations. Balancing your exit with daily operational priorities can be distracting and exhausting. I believe that implementation is where most business owners buckle under and can't get the deal done because, from their point of view, there are:

- Too many balls to keep in the air
- So many new once-in-a-lifetime decisions to make
- All the changes to make in the business, in their leadership and in their business model
- So many different experts to bring up to speed – all charging full rates
- All the contacts and negotiations that take longer than anticipated

Moreover, there's the loneliness and isolation of working through this process which takes years, especially when you try to do it alone. Help is available. Our clients at This Way Out Group LLC appreciate the support of a virtual partner at their side through the whole process to ensure they complete the transaction and transition to their reinvention.

Delegation To Add Value to Your Firm

So where can you delegate?

Nightingale Success is a weekly newsletter offered by Nightingale/Conant. Here's a quote from one issue

---

Too often leaders who lack the time to think strategically don't use the full potential of their employees. People who think they can do it better if they do it themselves, or feel they might lose control if they delegate, create more problems than they solve. – Tom Gegax

---

A key piece of the puzzle of leading a championship team is to learn to delegate effectively so that more of the detail tasks come off your plate, and the crises don't occur as often. Then strategic planning can take its rightful place as an important use of your time at the helm of your business since effective delegation frees you up for more important pursuits in this case, implementing your exit plan, which can raise profits and prepare the business for sale.

To make space in your schedule for the strategic effort of the exit process, it is essential to delegate day to day responsibilities to your team. When you delegate all day to day responsibilities, you are also transferring the value of the business from you to the business. This is one more way to make your business buyer ready and buyer attractive.

Here is a core skill set and process for delegation, with my observations.

1. **Completely Transfer Ownership** of tasks – Be very clear that you have relinquished ownership of that task/ responsibility, and that the monkey is on their back not yours any more.

2. **Explain Why** – Explain to employees why they are being asked to take on the assigned task – it cultivates support, confidence and initiative.

3. **Get Their Wheels Turning** – You must mentor or coach the delegate to develop an effective action plan, e.g. ask good questions or leading questions.

4. **Determine Deadlines** – A goal without a deadline is only a dream. Agree to a firm deadline to avoid any task slipping to the bottom of the employee's priority list.

5. **Ask for a ReCap** – Always double check, never assume perfect understanding. Listen carefully to what they heard – that's what they'll do. You may need to repeat this multiple times as each new project unfolds.

6. **Monitor – Do Not Hover** – When you delegate you have to let go, so don't defeat the purpose by micromanaging unless absolutely necessary (e.g. new employee, critical path **No Take-Backs** factors).

7. This is hardest for the leader who knows how to do the task in his sleep. The opportunity, when the first signs of trouble appear, is to patiently coach your employee back on track rather than usurping the project yourself.

8. **Play to Each Employee's Strong Suit** – Tailor assignments to people's strengths. Know who is a big-picture thinker and know who is superb with the details.

9. **Don't Duplicate** – When you delegate, don't overlap assigned tasks. If two or more people are involved, state clearly, up front, who's in charge.

10. **Distribute Evenly** – This takes some forethought, but you will build a stronger championship team if you delegate some challenges to promising less-tested people and not just rely on your star employees.

You can delegate individual tasks or you can delegate responsibility for an entire project. The more you delegate, the more time you free up for your more strategic responsibilities.

Set up processes for everything– even if you are the only one to follow the process. By writing them down, you no longer have to reinvent them every time they must be done. And as soon as you can delegate a process, it is in place and spelled out ready to give it away.

For each system, process, procedure you can get out of your head, standardized and on paper you will gain more time, not just once but every time that process needs to be repeated and you are adding proven measurable value to your business that will come back to you at the sale.

Automation

The bottom line with automation is that you work less and make more money. Automation tools can do the work much faster than any one person, all at the same time, and free up your time to focus on the strategic efforts to cash out of your business when you want to.

Automation is not just for the factory floor. You can automate:

- A marketing campaign, a newsletter or autoresponder series.
- A contact management system for any size company database
- Sales scripts, sales strategy, follow-up sequence
- Ordering supplies from a vendor
- Payroll

- Delivery schedules and delivery routes
- Environmental factors like lights, heat, air, sprinklers, door locks, cameras, etc.
- Technology upgrades, maintenance, and backups
- Telephone answering, appointment scheduling, online ordering

Anything that can be automated can also produce a report. You can better spend your time reviewing reports and deciding how to enhance an automated process, increase its value or decrease its cost, than repeating the process itself one more time.

Here are the three advantages of even the simplest level of automation:

1. You will create or setup each system once – You can run it many times – like your newsletter or infinitely, like a folder for a particular RSS feed.
2. For each task you identify to automate – you've also identified things that are duplicable and repeatable – which means they do NOT have to be done by you – more freed up time.
3. Automation de-clutters your desk, your computer desktop, your ToDo list,

Outsourcing, delegating and automating are skill sets that help you become a strategic entrepreneur turning your business into that wealth producing machine.

Knowledge

Knowledge, the third pillar is the combination of information you have or acquire, applied through the filter of your experience and expertise in your profession or industry.

Information + Experience = Knowledge

Knowledge + Insight = Wisdom

From all your experience and expertise in your own industry, you have amassed a body of knowledge that likely puts you in the category of a master.

When you integrate your knowledge with the insights gleaned from all your experience and research, you have built up unrivaled wisdom in your specialty.

However, in terms of your Knowledge, do you experience any of the following in your business?

- The whole business is in your head – only in your head.
- Don't know how to plan, when to plan, when to find time to plan
- No marketing plan, sales plan, financial plan or operating plans – except in your head
- Don't know how to automate or outsource
- No operating procedures established
- No contingency plans
- No exit strategy in place
- Keep all expertise in the owners/ executives heads and private files

> *If even one of these is true for you –*
> *it is a flag of what is holding back*
> *your business from all it could be.*

Indeed, in the real world, it is hard for your business to serve clients and make a profit, and address all these challenges at the same time. It's even harder if you are still wearing all the hats in your business, because the 'day to day doing' - gets in the way of focusing on and making time for the visionary, strategic leadership tasks that are essential to your long term goals.

In each area where you are not an expert you always have two choices:

1. Do what is necessary to acquire the mindset, skill set and knowledge to effectively deal with those obstacles or gaps.
2. Hire someone to do the job for you.

When you decide to exit your business, you have the same two choices. You can take the time to become an expert in all facets of how to sell a business (very costly, time consuming and unrealistic) or hire a team of experts to make it happen so you harvest the wealth in your business.

Transfer Your Knowledge

When you get ready to sell your business, the value cannot still be in your head and in your control. The value of the business must be in the business itself in order for it to be monetized and for a buyer to see the value without your active involvement.

Before you can sell the business for maximum value, you must transfer all your knowledge and wisdom into your team, systems, and procedures to carry on prosperously in your absence.

For each challenged listed above, here's what you need to do:

If/Then Solutions

- **The whole business is in your head – only in <u>your</u> head.**
  You must share every idea, policy, system, process, key, password, contract, etc. with your management team. You may give specific tasks and responsibilities to specific people or you can appoint a successor to take on your operational role.

- **Don't know how to plan, when to plan, when to find time to plan.**
  You must delegate day to day operations and make time to plan strategically. Both are necessary. They go hand in hand. Get training, hire an advisor, or hire a temporary COO to get plans in place.

- **No marketing plan, sales plan, financial plan or operating plans documented.**
  Get all these plans out of your head an on paper and assigned to different people to implement and achieve the goals in each area. Delegate responsibility for each area of your business to someone, not you. Make them operationally responsible, not you.

- **Don't know how to automate or outsource.**
  Exit planning is a great incentive to learn to automate and outsource to get more done, cheaper, not by you. Start by automating just one task. Start outsourcing by hiring an individual or a company to take over just

one task or project on your To-Do list. Decide no new tasks will get added to you To-Do list – instead you will always seek to delegate, automate or outsource first.

- **No operating procedures.**
  Create an Operations Manual. Buyers expect to be able to read your operations manual, instead of calling you for each procedure. Every time you do something that is a process or procedure, write it down. Every time you document or record how you do something, you are adding value to the business. Start by simply taking notes on an index card for each task, process, system, tool you use.

- **No contingency plans.**
  A contingency plan is like a security blanket for your business. It protects you, your business, your team and your customers. It also demonstrates to your buyer how valuable your business is that you are willing to protect everything that can be considered unique systems, models or intellectual property your intangible capital. You must lay out your emergency plans for fire, flood, other natural disasters, loss of power, computer crash, password security, data security and redundancy, safety and OSHA policies, backup procedures for when each person is on vacation, ill, let go, etc.

- **No exit strategy in place.**
  You must choose to take action to explore and consider exit options that would suit you. Take responsibility for ensuring the longevity of your

company, the legacy you can leave, and providing ongoing employment security for your team. By following an exit plan you will be in control of when you exit, on what terms and the valuation you will receive to fund your reinvention.

- **Keep all expertise in the owners/ executives' heads and private files.**
  You must start sharing your knowledge and wisdom in the business and about the business. You will maximize the value you will receive at exit, only if you transfer all of your knowledge and wisdom about the business to your team.

Everything on this list is a challenge all owners face to some degree. You can share your knowledge, understanding, wisdom and guidance willingly with your team and make your business an attractive buy at a premium price. Or you can horde all your knowledge, resist potential buyers' due diligence efforts to understand the value in your business, and struggle to sell the business for a fair return.

The good news is that we can all learn new mindset/attitudes and beliefs, we can all learn new skill sets, *and* we can all learn new information combined with experience to produce the knowledge we need.

PART III
Foundations for Growth and Value

The foundation for growth and value for your business starts with planning.

PLAN

The average business owner spends 80 hours
preparing a business plan and
only 6 hours preparing for their exit
ROCG 2007 Survey of Business Owners

That lack of preparation and planning is the reason why owners are ill-prepared to achieve an ideal exit from their business. Instead, they settle for only 50-70% of the value of their business when they sell.

It's up to you to maximize the value you can receive at exit. It's up to you, the owner, to demonstrate future value for the buyer, including growth projections to justify the selling price you want to receive on your terms.

You can delay and minimize your efforts and go for a sale that leaves 30-50% of the value of your business on the table or you can plan and strategize over time to prepare you, the business, and your team for the best possible outcome.

Exit planning starts with two exercises, one for you as the owner, and a parallel exercise for the business. In this exercise you document your personal core values, your vision and your mission (outlined earlier under Vision and Vales)

Repeat the exercise, with or without your management team, for your business.

With values, vision and mission in mind, you can start planning for your exit and what that will mean for the business as well.

By planning ahead, you can be more strategic with each hire, each goal, each decision you make between now and your target exit.

When you have a clear plan for your exit, you will make better decisions, easier, faster, with less risk, fewer mistakes and hit fewer deadends in every area of your business.

With an exit plan integrated into your business plan, corporate goals and strategy will be tied to your end goal, your personal end game.

To exit on your terms and timeline your plan should cover a wide range of issues, decisions and changes. This doesn't have to be expensive. But it takes concentrated time, effort, commitment and follow-through to see results. Here are a few areas to start at absolutely no cost.

Strategic Planning
Strategic planning is the art of direction and decisions. Building wealth and exiting your business don't start when you are closing in on the finish line. It's proven that when you focus on selling your business two to five years before initiating the sales process, you will almost certainly realize a much larger return. Developing a systematic approach to growth with a focus on

your long-term goals makes every decision along the way easier, even in the face of risk, incomplete information, or unexpected change.

Continuity/Succession Planning

Continuity and Succession Planning are the art of the changeover.

Your job here is to maximize the value you receive when you sell or transfer your businesses. A systematic approach to succession planning gives you control, choices and sufficient time to choose, train and transition management of your business. The more lead time you give yourself and your team to get up to speed on new roles and responsibilities, the easier it is for you to let go and move on.

Exit Planning

Exit planning is the art of monetizing our business.

Exit planning for wealth is all about maximizing and preserving the transferable value of your business. It's extremely important to integrate personal, financial and estate planning goals; and then coordinate them with the growth goals and opportunities of your business; to maximize profit and minimize tax liability on both sides. Your fiduciary objective is to transfer ownership and corporate value as profitably as possible. Take this responsibility seriously, early on, so you harvest the wealth in your business, not the tax man or others.

Contingency Planning

Contingency planning is the art of structuring your business for opportunities, possibilities and growth.

CEOs in general never take time to develop contingency plans. They are building a prosperous business not planning for a crisis or its demise. Skipping this one element of their business minimizes the value they can expect a buyer to pay for the business. You must develop those contingency plans and build the foundation elements to maximize valuation and make the business buyer ready.

Transition Planning

Transition planning is the art of reinvention.

When you stop and think about it, most entrepreneurs do not measure success in terms of the financial rewards, but rather by the freedom and potential legacy that these financial rewards confer. But entrepreneurs often postpone transition planning because they struggle with how they would use their new freedom and how they want to define their legacy. If that's you, transition planning helps you find new purpose, community, and structure for your time; and then how to master wealth management and its new opportunities, challenges and responsibilities.

What's Stopping You?

The majority of business owners avoid, procrastinate, deny, and postpone any discussion of business exit planning. The statistics consistently report 95% of all owners find excuses to not plan their exit.

The anticipated fear and overwhelm are exaggerated. When you put it in perspective, exiting your business is far easier and produces many more reasons for you to celebrate, than the U.S. military exit from Iraq.

No CEO Can Do It Alone
Just like it took large teams of experts and years to plan and implement the U.S. military exit from Iraq; you need to surround yourself with a team of experts who know more than

you do about exit strategies and achieving your exit objectives. You can then focus on what you do best in the business while your team streamlines the process of exiting your business on your terms and on your time line.

No Planning

The absence of planning is one of the deadliest oversights a CEO can succumb to. CEOs know better. They just don't invest the time and effort to plan their exit. The default option is that you will exit your business feet first or worse, close up shop with nothing to show for all your time, effort, expertise and resources invested. Too many CEOs resign themselves to never monetize their business, never fulfill their dreams or live their legacy.

Exit planning actually will make you more money, make the business stronger and more valuable; and provide your next steps beyond the business, that is, your reinvention after you leave.

Plan Your Exit Strategy By Design Rather Than By Default

Everyone starts their business confident in what they set out to do with a dream of what the business will provide for them. We all get very busy working in the business and it's natural to not worry about the future, never mind when and how you will exit the business. But if you are serious about cashing out of the business at some point in the future, here are the 5 first steps to ensure you achieve your goal to fulfill the promise of what your business would deliver for you and your family.

1. **Identify your exit strategy goal.**

    Do you want to build the business to a certain level and sell it? Do you want to pull a certain income out of the business until you die?   Do you want to pass the business on to your successor or a family member, or some other specified designee?

2. **What does the business have to do/provide/deliver – to allow you to achieve that goal**? –

It varies depending on what you want. Even if what you want is a moving target, document it anyway. You never know, an exit opportunity out of left-field could help you achieve your goal easier, better or quicker than what you planned. Keep your exit strategy front and center.

3. **What are the steps and milestones for that goal?** –

With the first 2 pieces in place, now you can start breaking down the steps it will take, and all the pieces you have to pull together. Some pieces like clean financial records and documenting all procedures can take years – well before you are in a position to act on your exit strategy. In this case, achieving your goal hinges on staying focused on the tasks that lead to realizing your ideal exit strategy.

4. **Which exit options appeal to you and which one will best fit your goal?**

Based on your goal of when to exit, how to exit, and what happens to the business when you do exit, etc.; the most effective exit strategies become obvious to achieve your goal. Others clearly don't fit your needs or objectives; and maybe others, you have no interest in pursuing. Only with a clear plan by intention starting now (yes now), can you ensure you'll achieve your big hairy, audacious exit strategy goal.

5. **What steps can you take every quarter and every year to set up your business for that exit strategy?** Now we get to implementation. To achieve your exit strategy goal, the longer the timeframe you have to implement the business foundation pieces, the more cohesive and functional they will be, independent of you. This is one more way to maximize the value of the business in the marketplace, making it a more attractive opportunity for buyers. Especially if part of your goal, by design, is to command the best price, then it is imperative that you integrate working on your exit strategy into all strategic planning every quarter of every year.

Apply these five steps to design your exit strategy by intention rather than by default. This commitment will move you consistently closer to a profitable exit. It's what you must do to optimize your business and help your broker, consultant, lawyers and other exit professionals to help you achieve your goal of fulfilling your ideal exit. Anything less and your exit will be by default, at minimum value, at the greatest cost to you, with the fewest choices and less leverage to achieve your goals and dreams beyond the business.

Structure and Your Exit Plan

When you implement a structure and build the resources to take on all the key roles in your business (human resources, assets, organizational structure, tools, services, etc.); they must be aligned with your exit plan. You are building a business to be in a position to exit that business on your terms.

If you built these elements of your business helter skelter, the business model may not be clear or clean, certainly not easy for a prospective buyer to discover.

Envision how the business will be managed (by others), the support team you need in place (adding more tangible value to the business), and the structure and systems that must be in place to make you superfluous to day-to-day operations.

This becomes your goal, to maintain or preferably grow revenues even as you remove yourself from day-to-day activities and decision-making.

Nothing else substitutes for implementation. Therefore, your vision statement and your exit plan becomes the bookends of implementation. They must agree strategically.

Don't Ignore Succession Planning

Along the lines of *'begin with the end in mind'*, start each new year with an eye towards identifying who will be your successor and how you will implement your succession plan – even if you anticipate it will be decades into the future.

My father's story I shared at the beginning of this book makes this point.

Identifying Your Successor

This is about securing business continuity. Many if not most business owners avoid, postpone and in the end fail to plan for their business continuity in the event they can no longer work due to death or illness.

- They subscribe to the naïve theory that they're too young to worry about succession or retiring or their exit strategy – even after age 65!
- They assume nothing will ever happen to them, they're too healthy, to vital and too important to the business. The logic they use is: "If I don't think about the 'what if's' – they can't happen..."

- They don't bother to create a business succession plan to address an unanticipated event such as disability or death – which can occur any time.

Ideally, every business owner should start succession planning and work himself or herself out of a job from the outset, even in the business plan .It's never too late to start today.

With an eye for hiring, grooming and cultivating successors in various aspects of the business, you have time to instill your strengths and values wide and deep throughout the organization.

For owners of small and medium size businesses, the business is a primary asset (up to 80% of their portfolio) they will need to liquidate to fund their retirement and provide for the financial future of their families.

If you intend to sell your business to a third party, then becoming detached from the day-to-day operations is a straightforward strategic process you need to put in motion, starting early.

As the seller, in order to maximize the value you can realize from the business and produce a financial gain, you must shift the value of the business from you personally, to the business itself. The sooner you start focusing on this long-term objective, the better the outcome for both you and the business.

Alternatively, if you wish or intend to keep the business in the family, your choices for successors can shift or be constrained by family requirements, needs and politics. These factors can be slow, complicated and even difficult to balance and resolve.

The time and effort you invest early and consistently to define, clarify, communicate and resolve successor issues will result in a stronger company, stronger team and a much more successful succession.

Succession planning is the responsibility of you the owner, not your management team or the next generation. You must develop your succession plan in sync with your own transition plan to balance the best interests of the company with all its employees, vendors and clients; and the requirements of you the exiting owner who needs capital to fund the rewarding lifestyle you deserve as the fruit of your labors.

Build a full succession plan document. Share it with the individuals involved or share it with the entire team, depending on relevancy. Don't keep it a secret. Don't keep it in your head. To fulfill your vision and mission, the team, especially the successors being mentored into new positions, need to know well in advance what your plans are.

Succession planning is only one piece you need in place for a strong integrated strategic plan which also includes operations planning, transition planning and contingency planning.

Succession Problems Impact Buyers, Sellers And The Transaction Experts In The Middle
As the baby-boomer generation ages, a multitude of succession problems are becoming evident. Each one compounds the effect of the others. Here are just a few that pertain to the small-medium size business market that you should take note of now:

- In both the US and in China the children of baby-boomers are much less likely to take on the family business.
- According to family business expert Frank Schneider, statistics reveal that only a third of family businesses are successfully transferred to the next generation.
- Recent research out of the Family Firm Institute and Babson University for Entrepreneurship report that

seventy percent of family businesses do not survive to the third generation.

- A survey by PricewaterhouseCoopers finds that one out of every two company owners plan to sell their business within the next 10 years.
- Many baby boomers have decided to step back and re-evaluate their lifestyles. A typical seller today is more likely to be in their 40s or 50s rather than their 60s or 70s, as was the case 10 to 15 years ago.
- People 55 or older own thirty percent of all businesses with employees.
- Businesses with employees are expected to grow in number by twenty-two percent every five years

According to David Fields, president of San Diego-based IBG Capital Markets:

The intersection of private equity money and baby-boomer demographics means that [we] can conservatively assume a threefold increase in transaction activity for companies with employees as boomers move into retirement.

As much as the statistics paint a picture of abundant opportunity for buyers and transaction experts, it's not the same for sellers. One report out of British Columbia, Canada states that only 10% of all deals actually get done. The rest languish because the seller is not prepared or the sellers wait until it's too late (when there's no value for a buyer in the business).

Reinforcing that principle, John Zayac president and founder of IBG Business Service, Inc. in Denver, CO, states:

> *The best advice I could ever give to the owner of a middle-market company is this: Plan for the sale of your business from the day you start it. Most business owners exit their business with less than six months of advanced planning, consequently receiving a mere 50 percent to 70 percent of the business' potential value.*
>
> *Appropriate planning, well in advance of a transaction, will allow a business owner to maximize company performance.*

The downside for sellers is that there is a window of opportunity before the supply of businesses exceeds demand. The vastly increased supply of small and medium-sized businesses available because of baby-boomer retirement/ reinvention will drive down valuations and give new leverage to buyers instead.

There are supply-demand implications of millions of businesses flooding the market in a concentrated period of time. Owners are not factoring these implications into their exit planning in terms of timing, valuations, opportunity, buyers or successors.

Management Succession Planning First Steps

Mortality is not my favorite subject either. But leaving a legacy in your business is a way to ensure immortality not possible anywhere else. An effective succession plan establishes the ground rules for what will happen when you are no longer around or no longer capable of managing the company's affairs. Here's where to start:

- To add value and make the business buyer attractive, consider appointing objective outsiders as members to your company's Board of Directors independent of ownership.

- Establish regular strategic planning meetings – annually, or better, quarterly - that include successors and key employees whom you need to stay fully engaged in the company.

- Select and regularly communicate with a team of outside advisors, including lawyers, accountants, consultants, wealth advisors, tax advisors and even brokers and valuation experts who have experience with privately held businesses, complex corporate matters and estate planning. These advisors can be a source of insight, continuity and strength as you prepare the business for succession or during an unexpected crisis.

- Be very honest with yourself when evaluating the strengths and weaknesses of candidates you consider as possible successors – internal or external. Try to separate issues of family, loyalty, and longevity from issues of business acumen and strategic leadership.

- Start early to be prepared for the unexpected. Most closely held businesses experience a "sudden loss" of leadership due to death or disability because the owner never planned or prepared for their transition to reinvention; thus leaving behind children or spouses ill prepared to continue to manage the business effectively or sell it most profitably. What would be your plan for the "following Monday morning?" Who would open the doors and run the company?

- Invest the time and money to train and educate the "next generation" of leadership for the company-whether the successor is your spouse, children or another family member or outside management hired in. If your succession plan calls for a full or partial sale of your business to some or all of your staff, do the same for the employees who will take over.

Family Business Succession Planning – A Special Case

Succession planning is a combination of contingency planning, management planning, hiring, transitioning out of an operational role, taking on a more strategic role, and looking ahead to your reinvention beyond the business.

In family businesses, succession planning may include determining ownership and management succession on independent parallel tracks.

Your exit plan should include the time and effort to implement succession planning and grooming, to ensure the company survives your departure. Your exit plan will likely be a critical part of your own financial and estate plans. Your future prosperity and endeavors may be linked to the future growth and profitability of the business you leave behind, not to mention peace and unity at family gatherings.

Four Issues Of Family Business Succession

The business succession plan is also your exit plan. Your succession planning process should begin as early as possible just like any other exit plan: ideally, when you buy or start the business.

The best business sale outcomes are never a fluke. That's even more true when your exit plan entails succession planning within the family. Five issues underscore effective family business succession. These issues apply to any size business regardless of industry.

Family business succession can be a complex process. The combination of personal and business interests, emotional and financial, are leading causes of conflict in family businesses and as a result, many families never address or resolve these issues ever. These issues are compounded with each generation. That's why you need to set out a formal pragmatic process for succession within the family, to secure the health and growth of the company, the right family members assume the reins of leadership, preserve your legacy and still ensure you can harvest the wealth from the business you built.

Here are some issues to be aware of when considering your own family business succession:

1. Are your children or other members of your family the right people to take over the business? When it comes to family, it can be very helpful to have a pre-defined rubric of objective criteria for the job as well as engaging independent external experts to facilitate this process. Ask yourself the following questions as objectively as you can:

   a. Do any of your children have the necessary skills, education and experience to take over running the business? If not, are they willing and capable of learning these skills? Outside training as well as mentoring may be required. Do they share your goals, values and aspirations for the business? Do not assume or minimize these cultural issues within the family or within the business.

b. Do any of your children actually want to take over the business? They may have very different ideas for their future or even different ideas for the business.

Open and honest discussions about these issues with family members can be extremely difficult and awkward for all concerned. Have the discussions anyway. Do not avoid them. Outside advisors can facilitate this process and open the communication to allow you to come to clear and effective solutions.

2. Communicate openly and honestly about your hopes and dreams for the business going forward. Ensure that you are not imposing your own goals and aspirations onto your children. And, when you do transition ownership/management/control of the business to family members, do so in a way that is fair and transparent. Otherwise, you risk alienating family members who do not participate.

3. Ensure that you have the appropriate business agreements in place, which are fair and contracted on commercial terms. One of your children may express a desire to take over the business while another wants to pursue their own professional goals.

Later, jealousies or rivalries may arise if the business does well and the child who didn't participate in the business feels unjustly treated. A proper agreement in place will protect everyone from any future potential claims that may be made against you and your estate.

Given the current high divorce rate, it may also be wise to consider an agreement to protect against claims made by your children's spouses against family business assets if their marriages break down.

4. Keep in mind that you do not necessarily need to pass your business on to your children in order to set them up to financially benefit from the business. This is an obvious statement, but one that is easy to overlook when your own identity, self-worth and sense of purpose and value have become fundamentally intertwined in your business. There are many options to ensure that future generations benefit financially that don't necessarily involve them shouldering the mantel of owning/running your business. This is particularly true if the children are not ready, interested or have the aptitude and commitment to take on running the business. They may have other plans and aspirations. Talk to your attorneys, wealth advisors and insurance brokers about options.

By passing the business on to your children, you could be putting yours and their entire financial future at risk if it's not a good fit. In contrast, if you were to sell the business and set your children up with financial structures funded by the sale proceeds, you would mitigate their risk, and they would have the flexibility to pursue other plans or aspirations.

By working on succession planning early, you can make it a smooth painless transition.

Contingency Planning

Contingency Plans

Murphy's Law – if something can go wrong, it will. The same is true for your business, as well as your exit from the business. Knowing this up front is another incentive to start early and aim for an early exit. You want to build a contingency plan for the business in the case of any crisis or emergency. Most important: you need an emergency plan documented with a copy kept totally offsite – if for any reason you can't get into your offices, you lose power and can't access computers or passwords, or there's a fire/blizzard/hurricane that destroys your business, etc.

Plans like these and plans for other types of unexpected situations should be built right into your business exit plan from the outset. You also need a documented contingency plan in case you, the owner/CEO, divorce, become physically or mentally disabled, have a heart attack/stroke and are laid up for six months or even worse, if you should die. This plan needs to include your thoughts and plans and financial decisions or commitments already made. Additionally, your contingency plan must include all current buy-sell agreements, services, resources, client orders, employee contracts, key employee incentive programs, business/disability/life insurance policies that are in effect.

This document grows in value the more you include in it. This document itself by residing on the shelf beside your governance documents, immediately adds value to your business for a potential acquirer. It is tangible proof that the business is not all in your head, that you are indeed replaceable and the business can continue in your absence.

It's not realistic to try to build a plan to deal with every possible contingency and disaster. Focus on documenting mission critical activities and the resources needed to keep them operating.

Goals of Your Contingency Plan
1. Minimize the impact on day-to-day operations
2. Contain/constrain the damage and define your response – so you can move on
3. Minimize the financial implications of any major event
4. Decide and document alternatives to continue operations, before they are ever needed

5. Assign and train team members on emergency procedures in the event of a crisis that is either company-wide (a blizzard or hurricane that wipes out power) or personal to you (a stroke or a broken leg).

6. Outlines steps, procedures, policies, responsibilities to resume operations rapidly.

Your contingency plan should include a copy of client and vendor contracts and be both accessible and secure. Ideally, it should include sections to address each element listed below.

Core Contingency Plan Elements

- Preparation & Response
- Recovery – Security, Safety, People, Data , Passwords and Keys
- Resources
- Emergency Contact Information – team, executives, board members, emergency services
- Identify essential personnel
- Contact communication procedures
- Publicity, public relations procedures and statements
- Insurance and broker information, copies of your contracts
- City, State & Federal Information and Telephone numbers
- Essential Department Responsibilities – and alternate assignments
- Supplies
- Budgeting and redundancies to prepare for emergencies
- Vendors contract terms and phone numbers
- Redundant systems for inventory, records, confidential data and files

- Steps to regroup/rebuild an integrated system of physical plant, power systems and technology from a cold start
- Ongoing effective working collaborative supporting relationships to facilitate communications, public relations, and politics
- Client list/duplicate database
- Identify potential risks and issues as well as solution options., with a process to move on
- Recovery/Return Team

Once drafted, your contingency plan is a working document to be reviewed and updated at least annually. Its existence adds tangible value to your business. Keep it secure. Your contingency plan should be signed by you the owner and any necessary witnesses. Keep a copy in-house, a second copy with your legal advisor and a third copy offsite where your key executives and officers know where it is and how to access it. For some companies, keeping it in the cloud will suffice.

Is Your Business Ready To Be Sold?

Are You Ready To Sell Your Business?

I repeat: Are you ready to sell your business? Is your business ready to be sold?

These are not the same question although the answers must be consistent.

Have you thought about the former but assumed the latter to be true?

Are you prepared to let go of your business, to get out now? Physically? Logistically? Financially? Emotionally? That's a series of discussions right there that you must address before you can sell your company. Those are questions you will address as your team, your broker and your family ask them.

But What About The Business Itself?

What have you done to make the business buyer ready or buyer attractive?

What have you done to prepare the business not just you for this transition? You may be clear and prepared for your transition, but your business will transition to new ownership in a financial or strategic sale. Is it ready? These transitions can be easy or very tough.

For the business itself, if you leave your reinvention as a black hole and/or don't communicate with your relevant staff, you set up the sale of the business to fail. Allowing the business and your team to transition smoothly and successfully to new ownership is your responsibility. Indeed, that successful smooth transfer is a key to the value a buyer will be willing to pay for.

To make the business transition easy, you must prepare the business to be an attractive asset for the buyer. Below are eight questions to consider to ensure an easy and profitable sale when you exit the business.

Is Your Business Ready to be Sold?

1. **Do you have a history of consistent sales and profit growth?**
   Documented history of sales, profits and growth which you can show buyers provides proof that can be used at valuation. At least two years' worth, preferably longer.

2. **Do you have at least 2 years of clean financials?**
   Your bookkeeper and accountant don't see the whole picture. You have other tangible and intangible assets and contracts. All of these will be reviewed and valued. You can't hide anything from buyers or brokers. You can't afford to.

3. **Do you have a foundation of robust systems, processes and structure and are they fully documented?**

Does your business run on consistent processes and procedures or do you run it out of your head? For the business to be ready to be sold, all systems, structure and strategies must be documented.

4. **Do you have projections showing increasing value for the buyer long after you exit?**

Buyers will not pay for an old tired business on its last legs. They want to know there's more life, more opportunity for them to make a good profit for years after your exit. Can you prove that opportunity?

5. **Are you ready to make the necessary changes to make the business buyer attractive?**

How much time, effort, and expertise will you invest back into the business now, as you get ready to move on? Are you willing to set the business up for even greater success without you at the helm?

6. **Do you know what makes your business buyer attractive?**

You must know what it is about your business that makes it valuable enough for someone else to buy it. This is the biggest sale of your life - selling the business you built.

7. **Do you know what makes your business successful in your market?**

Be sure the value is in the business and not just in you the owner.

8. **Are all your stakeholders prepared for the transaction?**

Just because you are prepared for the exit transaction on

your terms and you've planned your transition to reinvention, - doesn't mean all your stakeholders are on the same page with you. Before you get to the transaction, be sure all business stakeholders support the transaction so you indeed can make a successful exit from the business.

Many owners prepare themselves for their exit and forget to prepare the business resulting in a tough transition for the business, clients, team, and suppliers.

These challenges are totally avoidable if you prepare the business for the exit transaction while you prepare yourself for your transition to reinvention.

Getting Out - Have You Prepared A Transition Plan?

Preparing a written transition plan is a critical element of your whole exit strategy. But surveys consistently verify that CEOs avoid this element regardless of age, or size of the business. There's a concerted dearth of attention by CEOs as to how they will transition out of the business, never mind determining to what they are transitioning.

Most owners:

- Fail to get the highest possible value for their business, or
- Transfer it to an ill-prepared successor, or
- End up paying too much in taxes

or even all of the above.

Whatever your goals or your timeline, it is time to plan for your exit now. Experts agree that if you want to maximize the value from all your sweat equity, you must invest in proper planning years in advance of your intended exit.

1. The 2007 ROCG Survey Report results confirm there is an overall lack of planning. Their survey found that only 9% of business owners have a formal written plan that includes succession and transition planning for the business. That means 91% of all CEOs in the US have no plan of how to transition out of day to day operations.
2. Based on the 2010 Census numbers, current estimates report that more than 40% of business owners plan to exit within the next five years; and 80% of all business owners plan to exit within the next ten years.

    But on a timeline of market trends, there will be many more sellers than buyers in the market place from 2013 – 2018 – just when that first 40% are expecting to sell their business.[1] Owners who delay planning until after their business has peaked, will not only find it harder to sell, take longer to sell and be squeezed by greater competition; they will also reduce their leverage and the resulting multiples they can cash out of the business.

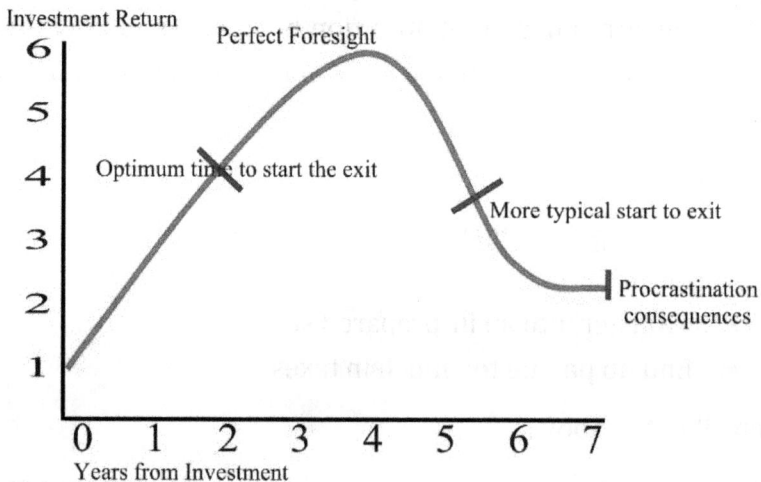

---

[1] Business Transition/Succession – The Increased Risk of Incurring Catastrophic Losses and What You Can Do To Avoid Them, October 2008, ROCG Americas LLC

It is a disaster waiting to happen. It will only be compounded when you add in the fact that 21million baby boomers will be selling off their businesses over the next 15 years.

Will Widespread Catastrophic Losses Be The Result?

Without proper advance planning, we could see wave after wave of business owners fail to harvest the wealth they need for their reinvention. These owners:

- May not be in position to maximize their personal finances for financial independence when they sell sale;
- May be forced to sell at a deep discount or accept unfavorable conditions;
- May risk a business closure, leaving them with nothing;
- May have a business that ultimately fails and/or potentially destroys family harmony in the transfer to family members.

Timely transition planning is a core strategy to avoid facing these types of obstacles and despair. Pro-active strategic business planning and transition planning can help to ensure that the transition is successful at meeting all the owner's goals for the business as well as lifestyle and legacy objectives.

Your Stakes Are High! Can You Afford Not To Get This Right?

You know the stakes are high - the highest, since your business is likely the most valuable asset you have and intend to monetize.

Then why do over 90% of all businesses avoid exit planning and do not have their transition plan documented? There is a mythical belief that business owners are invulnerable. There is an apparent universal belief that they can always do it tomorrow, that it's too early to plan their exit.

But without a plan, you are leaving everything to fate, when time takes its toll. The statistics bear out what I've been seeing for years; brilliant successful, industrious business owners are frozen in inaction on this one area of their business that they do not want to address. Even knowing how much is riding on the result (taking care of a spouse, children, grandchildren, other family members, partners, employees, customers, suppliers, and others), they still leave their legacy and their future lifestyle to chance.

In 2007, Mass Mutual did an American Family Business Survey. Their results, seem to substantiate this lethargy. *"Almost a third [of business owners] have no plans to retire, ever; and nearly another third report that retirement is more than 11 years away. Since the medium age of the current leaders is 51, **this means that many people plan to die in office...**"*[2]

Also in 2007, PricewaterhouseCoopers released a report on Canadian businesses succession plans, which found a lack of planning by owners that were 50 and over. They reported that, "many owners seem unwilling to seriously look into options to transition ownership before they are forced, by age or illness, to give up the business."

The second overall top reason given on both surveys was *'it's too time consuming.'*

Could this be the trigger point that will help drive owners into action?

---

[2] MassMutual Financial Group, Cox Family Enterprise Center Coles College of Business Kennesaw State University, The Family Firm Institute, Inc. (FFI), American Family Business Survey, Study: Family businesses growing steady and strong but face future risks, 2007

As in your on-going operations, succession and transition planning is about business strategy. It is about creating a structure that will help you organize your systems, structure, and processes, which in turn will help you increase the value of the business, and provide you a vehicle to smoothly transition your business to new ownership while you cash out on your terms.

Reinvention is the Time to Reap the Rewards of Your Harvest

Before you can implement that transition to reinvention,–you must have a plan for how you will engage your mind and fill your time for at least the next 365 days. Not just a broad brush idea, but rather a full-fledged plan with goals, milestones, projects to consume you. This will take time to explore and prepare. This plan must be tested and validated in the years leading up to your exit. It is essential that you lay out this plan before you complete the transaction

Whatever your definition of reinvention is, you must have a plan. You must write it out. You must build out the plan to consume your time, energy and passion for at least the next year. And you must test that plan for 2-4 weeks at a time at least once a year (aka vacation from the business you are preparing to exit).

Every hour you invest in your reinvention plan (like a business plan for your future) three to five years before your exit, will pay dividends in satisfaction, pleasure, fulfillment and security in the decades beyond your business.

What's Required on the Legal Side of Exit Planning and Execution?

Just like exit questions we discussed above, there's a whole set of legal elements, preparation, documents, asset/stock/cash mix trade-offs for buyers/sellers, the process sequence, real estate, closing,, agreements and Closing Package that you need to prepare and work through to make your business buyer ready at the closing.

I've compiled a simple list of documents, decisions and pieces you need before you can transfer ownership of your business. Some you can prepare early, along the way. Some are only needed in the last months of the transaction process itself.

I'm not an attorney. This list of what's needed is just to get you started when you seek out appropriate attorneys for your exit planning team. You may need to hire specialists in each area, depending on how unique your situation is. The attorney who helped you start the business, the attorney who prepared your divorce, the attorney you use for real estate transactions is likely not the specialized attorney you need to prepare your business for exit or to take you through the negotiations.

Agreements including confidentiality /non-disclosure/non-solicitation agreements with everyone, including:

- Customers
- Vendors
- Employees
- Competitors

Advance Preparation checklist:

- Confirming asset ownership
- Identifying intellectual property
- Protecting intellectual property
- Check for liens

- Corporate entity definition, location and status
- Review, Complete, Update all corporate documentation including:
  - Annual reports
  - Corporate minutes
  - Tax filings
  - Assess, revise and develop continuity contracts covering:
  - Key management and employee contracts
  - Vendor contracts
  - Key customer contracts

  that extend beyond your exit and that add value to the business.

- **Deal with any legal skeletons that are there**. If they are there, you must resolve them before talking to potential buyers because **the buyer will find them** during due diligence.

Explore and translate **the asset vs. stock deal** in the actual exit option you choose.

- What is good for one party is not always good for the other party
  Ex: in a stock sale, the buyer is buying shares of a company along with the liabilities – which will require more due diligence
  Ex: in an asset deal, you as the seller may retain ownership of the company while the buyer buys specific assets required to run the business.
- Define the agreement and understanding on the use of the name, brand, use of a name – especially if the brand is tied closely with the use of a family name

- An asset deal may require contracts, other documents and due diligence in order to transfer ownership

Processes To Bring Your Business Sale Transaction To Closure

- Non-binding Letter of Intent (LOI)
- Purchase Agreement – including
  - Representations and warranties and survival of those representations and warranties
  - Indemnification
  - Arbitration provision
  - Allocation
- Due Diligence
- Contingency dates
- Closing event and transaction

Due Diligence Review will include:

- Importance of other members of the exit team
- Current, pending or potential litigation
- Skeletons – if they exit, the buyer will ferret them out
- Environmental issues and implications
- Regulatory restrictions
- Non-compete agreements
- Vendor and Client Contracts
- Employment agreements with key management and employees and the impact/implications for the seller
- Review of **Real Estate** status
  - Owned
  - Leased
  - Mortgaged
  - Contracts
  - Part of the sale
  - Separate deal

Closing Event/Closing Transaction Package Preparation

- Ensure seller's security in any earn-out, employment agreement or promissory notes
- Non-compete agreements clear, agreed, up-to-date and countersigned
- Employment agreements clear, agreed, up-to-date and countersigned
- Documenting the conduct of business pending the exit event

This is just one area where it is apparent that you just can't work through all this alone to attain your ideal exit. Note the scope of what the attorneys can do. It is important to recognize that even with the right attorney at your side, the two of you can't do it all. You need a whole team of trusted advisors, not just one.

STAGE

Everyone knows what it means to 'stage your home'. It's about making your home ready and appealing to buyers so they'll offer your asking price.

Similarly, it's up to you to prepare your business to ensure you can showcase it in the best light, indeed making your business buyer ready and buyer attractive.

The easiest way to summarize what this will take is with systems. The word itself often repels people – they think systems require too much extra work. In fact, the whole principle behind systemizing is to create systems that make things run easier, smoother, cheaper; simpler and smarter.

The dictionary definition of systematize is: to arrange in accord with a definite plan or scheme; to order systematically.

When you systematize any thought or activity into a repeatable process, you have the clarity to teach and delegate that task or responsibility to someone else. You maintain control because you designed the system; but you are now free to focus on higher priorities and more strategic opportunities because a myriad of tasks and activities can be outsourced, automated or delegated.

Every time you establish a new system or process that does not have to be done by you and which is documented, you are adding value to the business for a prospective buyer. Every system, task, process, decision tree that you lay out in a repeatable form can be monetized for negotiating the value of your business when you want to exit.

Concept and Theory

The concept is simple. Look around your business and evaluate how everything is done. Once you find out how well something works, give it more weight, more value in your overall system, or less. If it doesn't work, eliminate it, modify it, or reinvent it. In this context, Staging is the process of integrating all your successful activities across the entire enterprise into a business strategy that is optimal for you in your business:

1. Measure and evaluate the results produced by each component in your strategy. Then look ahead to project and anticipate the implications, so you can track expected and actual results. You can better forecast the impact of your decisions when you know consistently that when you do *abc*, you'll get *xyz*.

2. If you decide a component of your system works well and you want to emphasize it more, before you implement that decision, always ask:

   What are the implications if you do, if you don't?

   The answers will reveal your best decisions. Each time you take the time to produce definitive answers, you will also establish tactics, best practices, and parameters to incorporate into your business strategy. This pattern will become a cycle you can apply in every area of your business.

3. Staging the business with systems is a commitment to transition from a tactical approach to business to a strategic approach to how things get done. Optimize your business strategy to add value to the business, and make it easier for prospective buyers to see and recognize that value; because your systems,

processes, and documentation are another way to showcase your most effective resources, strengths and assets.

4. Enhancing and enabling each department of your business with the tools and processes to systematize does not happen overnight. It's not always obvious. If an element of your staging efforts doesn't prove profitable the first time you try it, or the first time you put it on the market; don't reject it out of hand and go back to old familiar ways. Look at the results you've tracked and ask:

Is there another way I can apply this method/tactic and make it work in this business?

Often, there are new, state-of-the-art ideas you never knew, or cared to know, that will enhance the value of your business for your future buyer. Are you investing the effort, time and expense to systematize this department, this process, this product line to accelerate sales, to increase profit margins or to be buyer ready? If so, then in the context of your exit, persistence to master this new system, method or approach and refine it to work smoothly will add value to the bottom-line in the short-term and the long-term.

The systemization it takes to stage your business for your exit, is a leadership skill set you'll improve and master by doing. As you activate systems and upgraded systems throughout your enterprise, notice what this does for you as a strategic CEO. The discipline of systematizing decisions, processes and tactics is a skill set which clarifies your long-term goals and streamlines efforts to achieve bigger results in the business and beyond. .

Practical Context

Let's put this into practical terms. I know you're questioning if it's worth all the effort, change, chaos and risk to your current operation to implement new systems across the board. It is work. It is change. However, keep in mind, every change has the explicit measurable purpose of accelerating growth, increasing profits and maximizing the value of your business. When they can see the value that you know is in this business, they will be more receptive to paying what you think it's worth!

Here are a few ideas for systemization in the core areas of your business that will enhance the value of your business, staging your business to be buyer attractive.

Departments and Disciplines	Range of Systems
Sales	• Sales Funnel • CRM System • Sales Manual • Pricing Schedule • Sales Training System • Sales Goals and Monitoring Programs • Upsell and Downsell Options • Key Performance Indicators
Marketing	• Marketing Funnel • CRM System • Marketing Strategy • Marketing Tactics • Marketing Schedule • Key Performance Indicators • Marketing Budget
Finances	• Control of all finances (all assets) • Contract Management • All Accounts In Order • Projections and Forecasts • All Accounts Ready For Due Diligence
Operations	• Operations Manual for every area • Contingency Plans • Security/Emergency Planning • Facilities and Equipment Planning • Tracking and Measuring for every System/Process Implemented

Departments and Disciplines	Range of Systems
Administration	• Legal documents up-to-date and organized • Governance documents current, up-to-date, in order, organized • Management and Staff contracts up-to-date, signed and ready to transfer • Leadership and Continuity Plans defined and documented • Board of Directors and Board of Advisors charter, responsibilities and roles • Time Management Systems And Training • Productivity Systems and Training • Continuity Plans • Succession Plans
Strategy/Planning	• Business Plan • Strategic Plan • Succession Plan • Transition Plan
Customer Service	• Customer Experience Systems • Customer Loyalty System • Service Systems, Response And Resolution • Customer Service Training Systems • Customer Service Evaluation/Improvement Systems
Intellectual Property	• Identify and documents all IP • File all trademark and patent applications • Clarify and document ownership of all IP (individual or the business • Document the corporate definition of IP ownership as it applies to your exit

Entrepreneurs by nature resist systemization. As an incentive to implement systems throughout your business, let's look at the benefits of using systems and processes.

Why You Must Institute Systems And Processes

When you **systematize** every area of your business, you will:

1. Stay very organized and free up more time

   - Have more time to lead instead of manage
   - Gain control in ways you never thought possible
   - Regain control in ways you thought you'd have to hire a large staff to do for you
   - Organize every area of your business

2. Streamline activities

   - Streamline how you run your business to add value and reduce stress
   - Immediately be able to book multiple vacations this year
   - Never reinvent the wheel again

3. Increase efficiencies

   - Eliminate mistakes
   - Eliminate late and incomplete work
   - Open up your business for accelerated growth
   - Gain easy access to the reports you need
   - Drastically increase the value of the business

4. Get more done

   - Streamline work to get done easier and faster
   - Teach your team once and stop using your most valuable asset (your time) re-teaching them

5. Move things off your plate

   - Give tasks and responsibilities to others, so you can take a vacation or explore your reinvention options

- Make better decisions sooner and faster than you thought possible
- Radically reduce your risk running the business
- Measurably enhance the value of your business

When you measure these efficiencies, you'll see *time savings* and opportunities to *get more done*. When you apply systems in any area, the third or triple bottom line is that you'll also *save money* while increasing your future valuation.

The real secret to all these systems and benefits is to:

1. Implement tools that help you get the results you know are possible in your business

2. Use those systems and tools consistently, and insist your team use them too. Institutionalize them into your corporate culture – even if you are a company of one.

3. Get your business out of your head

4. Track your results

5. Periodically schedule a review to measure the impact in every area of your business.

How Does Systematizing Help You Accelerate Growth And Maximize Value?

The most notable businesses that we remember and talk about are not the thousands of businesses that get started each year. Rather they are those enterprises that look like and act like a thriving business entity. Those businesses that survive, flourish and grow are distinctive in a number of areas, and one of the mail areas is strategic entrepreneurship. As a direct result of systematizing their businesses, strategic entrepreneurs build a buyer ready and buyer attractive business. You can too:

1. Run your business as a business with goals, budgets, strategy, campaigns, customer-centric, attentive to market trends and outside influences.

2. Keep accurate current financials. Do not run the entire business out of the checkbook. Operate the business so that it can withstand a complete audit.

3. Use credit and debt responsibly to grow the business because it's built into your strategic plan.

4. Take direction from your Boards. Learn to leverage your Board of Directors and Board of Advisors wisely. In your strategic plan you documented how to use your boards and trained your boards from the beginning.

5. Are responsive to the market because you have systems in place to monitor the prospect market, the competition and outside influences.

6. Build a strong team of experts around you by expecting everyone to document standards and systems in their area of expertise from inception. That way, company value is evident and not dependent on one individual.

7. Master the art of delegating, outsourcing, and automating in every area of your business– because you have recorded every process, policy and system to be repeatable by someone else.

8. See your productivity escalate by adhering to these systems. Your team will emulate your use of systems and get more done too.

9. With governance, legal documents and forms always up-to-date – your business is always ready for an eager buyer's due diligence.

10. With growth forecasts and goals in hand, you can anticipate capital requirements and capital expenditures and develop attractive options and minimize risks.

11. Implement new systems designed for the company to grow into, replacing systems you've outgrown that are holding you back.

12. Are very resilient and responsive because you always have a Plan B for every eventuality.

13. All your short-term and long-term decisions and goals are always tied to what it would take to fulfill your Exit Plan.

Use this list as your own checklist to build a foundation of systems in every area of your business. If you are not actively executing systems to gain these benefits, start now.

Systemization is what Staging is all about to accelerate growth and maximize value in your business. Systemization is a critical aspect of grooming the business for sale. It takes time to plan, decide, implement and monitor results of your strategic systemization. You will develop Key Performance Indicators to evaluate and refine these systems. When you package up those same Key Performance Indicators as a trends report with 2-3 years data - it becomes powerful proof to persuade your buyer of the value they are buying.

How Can A CEO Grow The Business And Plan The Exit At The Same Time?

At first glance, it may appear to be a futile contradiction for a CEO to try to grow the business and plan the exit at the same time. But when you look at them side by side, you'll see that growing the business is an essential early phase of any exit plan. The mistake is trying to look at them as sequential projects instead of concurrent projects. The requirements of one will guide the decisions of the other and vice a versa.

1. By increasing new revenues (a benefit to potential buyers) **growth** itself becomes a saleable asset

2. **Increased revenue from growth** is easy to measure and monetize to assess value for a potential sale.

3. When **decisions are made that lead to growth**, immediate goals are met. When those same decisions are aligned with the long-term goal of how you will exit the business, those decisions have greater strategic value.

4. **Test every decision** - When the long-term goal of your exit is known throughout the leadership team, every decision can be tested against these long-term criteria before implementation.

5. There are **many options** to consider when you want to grow your business. The options you select have a direct impact on your exit strategy and timeline. And if the exit plan is in place, all options for growth can be sorted to align business growth with your exit plan. Here are just a few basic options to use individually or in combination:

   - Increase sales prices
   - Increase new sales
   - Increase volume of sales/customer
   - Increase add on sales
   - Increase life of each customer
   - Open new markets
   - Open new channels
   - Increase capacity (sales, marketing, customer support, production, facilities)
   - Reduce costs
   - Reduce overhead

6. The forethought and documented strategic planning you invest to grow the business develops depth within the entire management team. That depth in leadership as well as the resulting measurable growth increase, adds value to the business that is very attractive to buyers.

Who's On Your Exit Team?

Whether you currently surround yourself with a strong team of advisors or not, when you start planning your exit, they are essential to every goal you want to achieve in this exit transaction.

Meet The Team Members You Need to Achieve Your Exit to Reinvention

Most business owners are not prepared to exit their own business. More than likely, that includes you. It's not your fault. No one taught you. No one showed you how to prepare for your exit. In fact, no one is really talking about any other parameter of your business except income.

Why Are You (Still) In Business?

Are you in business to produce income to pay yourself, or enough to cover payroll? Or are you in business to make a profit?

If you intend your business to make a profit, that means you expect to monetize the business at some point to produce the wealth you need for your reinvention.

When you decide you are ready and committed to an exit strategy, only then can your exit transaction team go to work on your behalf.

You're familiar with the phrase *"It takes a village to raise a child"*. The analogy fits your exit planning well. It takes a team to exit your business successfully.

Here's a brief list of experts you must consider for your exit team and their possible contributions.

Attorneys

Until now, most likely, one attorney was enough for your business affairs. For your exit, you want to raise the bar and engage very precise experts.

IP Attorney – You want an intellectual property attorney to help you identify, document and protect the unique ideas, processes, products and services you provide. Your IP attorney is a powerful expert resource to help you recognize and protect the real value in your business in the form of copyrights, trademarks, patents and other forms.

Business Attorney – Your business attorney is an expert on business and commercial transactions and contracts. This person or team understands corporate contracts, hiring practices, and negotiations as well as U.S. and state specific commercial law.

Governance Attorney – Your corporate governance is a system of structuring, operating and controlling the company with a view to achieve long-term strategic goals that satisfy all stakeholders, and comply with all legal and regulatory requirements. To be buyer ready, you need a legal team to review, update or correct and document your corporate governance practices, processes, customs, policies, laws, resolutions and institutions including the relationships among stakeholders such as shareholders, board of directors, employees, customers, creditors, suppliers and the community. According to Gabrielle O'Donovan, in *A Board Culture of Corporate Governance*, "the perceived quality of a company's corporate governance can influence its share price as well as the cost of raising capital." Your corporate governance is a system of structuring, operating and controlling the company with a view to achieve long-term strategic goals that satisfy all stakeholders, and comply with all legal and regulatory requirements.

Personal Attorney – You must bring your own personal attorney into the exit transaction to protect your own interests. You are this attorney's client. YOU hire this attorney to watch out for your best interests through the exit process. The business hired the business attorney to protect the business' interests, not yours. He/she cannot adequately serve in both roles.

Estate Attorney – You need your estate attorney to be an integral player in the discussions of your exit options to voice the legal impact on your estate of each choice and protect your long-term best interests.

Financial Experts

Business CPA – You need your business accountants putting the books in order for valuation and in a form that is buyer-attractive, showing off the business in the best light.

Personal CPA – You need your personal accountant to focus on your own accounts, or accounts to be set up prior to the exit transaction.

Chief Financial Officer – Even if you've never had anyone in this role, you need a chief financial officer(CFO) looking at the strategic financial impact of every marketing, financing, or growth decision leading up to your optimal exit option. Your CFO can bring valuable advice, expertise and insight to the process leading up to your exit. In addition, just by having a seasoned professional in the role adds value to the business that is appealing to prospective buyers.

Tax Advisor - You need your personal tax advisor to be an integral player in the discussions of your exit options to voice the tax impact on you of each choice and protect your long-term best interests.

Wealth Advisor – Your wealth advisor can help you fulfill your ultimate goals, live the lifestyle of your dreams, and leave a legacy and a dynasty. They can offer the best advice and opportunities if you include them in the discussions early – before you've made your exit choices. They can set up accounts in advance ready for you to utilize to maximum advantage at exit.

Transaction Experts

Depending on the size of your business, the type of business and the type of sale you are pursuing, you will want to use different transaction experts. They bring experience, connections, process and negotiating skills to the exit transaction that are irreplaceable for a successful exit.

Business Broker – A business broker assists buyers and sellers of privately held small businesses in the buying and selling process. They will value the business, advertise it for sale, interface with initial buyer inquiries and interviews, discussions, and negotiations. They facilitate due diligence and generally assist with the sale of the business.

M&A Advisors – Mergers and acquisitions is a specialized field of corporate strategy, finance and management dealing with the buying, selling, dividing and combining of different companies to help an entity grow rapidly in some way. M&A advisors, as a sub-niche of investment bankers, do not provide financing. They can find buyers and help you close the transaction.

Investment Bankers – If your business is large enough and the exit transaction is large enough or complex, you may need to work with an investment banker. Investment banks assist in raising capital or acting as your agent to issue securities.

Others

Business Partners – Your partners, whether they are currently active or silent in the business, must be part of the exit planning discussions. Your final plan must consider their concerns and or they can destroy your whole exit.

Life Partners/Spouse/Family – Your business exit and your reinvention plans affect them too. Your exit must take these people into consideration too. Include them in your decision-making to ensure a positive transition to reinvention with them.

Exit Strategist – You need someone focused on the strategic side of planning, systematizing, growing the business , someone who will help prepare you to move into a more strategic role to sell well, and someone who will help you explore and prepare for your exit and reinvention. You need an exit strategist who works with you on all levels through the whole process, who can also coordinate and facilitate your entire team of exit experts.

Valuation Experts – .Valuation is not a one-shot deal at the end with a buyer at the table. A history of value enhancements and the resulting increase in business valuation assessed annually, adds weight to a seller's position at a higher valuation.

Marketing consultants – You may want to bring other experts in early too, to maximize the value of the business to the buyer.

Staffing consultant – You may want to hire in key players/ successors to make the business more attractive to the buyer. You may need help finding people to fill these key rolls.

Human Resource (HR) consultant – An HR consultant can help you formalize your corporate culture and tie your team to the company, beyond your exit to secure their future with the company under the new owner.

I hear you saying: *"But I've never needed all these people before, why do I need them now, when I'm getting ready to get out of business?"* It's a normal knee-jerk reaction to resist engaging so many people. Nonetheless, you need the full team of experts now to:

1. Build a strong deep foundation
2. Accelerate growth
3. Protect all intellectual property
4. Get all governance up-to-date and compliant
5. Get the books meticulously clean, ready for an audit and due diligence
6. Maximize valuation
7. Get your accountants, tax advisor, estate attorney and wealth advisor on the same page – early
8. Expand exit options
9. Ensure the business is buyer ready
10. Transition your role from operational to strategic demonstrating that the value is in the business, not you
11. Prepare you, your team, your family for your exit
12. Prepare you and your family for your reinvention
13. Document and codify every system, strategy, process and procedure in the business.

It does cost money to exit well. Start early and you spread that cost over time. Staging the business to be attractive to your ideal acquirer or to successfully transition the business to your successors will deliver massive results in revenue and growth now, not just when you cash out. The return on investment of building and using your all-star exit team will multiply too

Wait until the last six months when you are tired and 'need' to get out fast, and you'll spend the same amount of money out of current revenues, reducing your best year numbers that a buyer is focused on. In the last six months, you don't have time to make improvements that you can monetize.

The cost to you, your legacy and your family will be compounded and the possible returns reduced, if you abdicate and don't act now.

When you surround yourself with experts to support the process, your business will be stronger, demonstrate appealing growth projections, will have a higher valuation than otherwise possible, and become buyer attractive. As a result, you can and will be able to exit your business by intention on your terms instead of closing the doors with no monetary gain by default.

Baby-Boomer Sellers' Opportunity

Here's the reason you can't afford to wait. You must plan y your exit now. Starting in 2013, the market will be flooded with businesses for sale as aging Baby-Boomers start exiting. It's a potential boomtown of businesses changing ownership.

Here's the recipe to have the licensed transaction experts competing to sell your business and have buyers eager to buy your business on your terms on your timeline:

- Start succession planning early
- Maximize valuation
- Accelerate growth
- Plan an early exit
- Make your business buyer attractive

It's worth the time invested along the way to be able to exit with the financial freedom to pursue your reinvention.

DRIVE

*Leverage is a vitally important fundamental concept that is
central to your dealmaking success.*
~ Jay Abraham

You built your business and now you want to monetize the value you know is there. This is when your team of experts help to execute the exit transaction; to ensure that buyers can see the true value of your business, and you can successfully complete the transaction and transition to your reinvention.

Driving the process is a full time job. Leading your business to its best year yet with strong projections for the future is your primary full-time job. That's why you need an exit strategist to facilitate this team to coordinate, collaborate and cooperation in your best interest and complete the transaction, while you ensure the business delivers the best opportunity for your ideal buyer/acquirer.

Your Real Wealth Isn't In Starting Your Business

You **will** never realize your real wealth by starting your business.

In fact, your wealth won't be made simply by growing your business either. The bottom line is that your real wealth will only be made from the profits of selling your business. Your best option is when you can sell to someone who will pay a premium for your business because they [the prospective buyer/acquirer] believes they can generate even more value from the business you've worked so hard to build.

The most successful entrepreneurs create plans that layout their roadmap to grow their business so they can exit [get out]

140

for the maximum valuation (dollar amount value) within a specified time period.

You can too because when you build a business with your exit in mind (whether via an internal/external sale, IPO or an acquisition), you set very different strategies and goals from the outset than when you simply try to 'grow' a business.

You see, your short-term results and success, and your long-term results and success are NOT mutually exclusive. When you build your business with a strong foundation **including** a defined exit plan, you can maximize short-term revenues and profits, while building and aligning your company for that multi-million dollar exit on your terms.

Since 1999, we have been developing exit strategy plans for our clients. Importantly, many of these clients who executed these plans, have since realized their high dollar exit dreams, which they had not previously known they could achieve. They are fulfilling the precise lifestyle dream they had when they first launched their businesses.

Your real wealth isn't in starting your business.
It's in how you exit.

Tracking And Measuring is How You Leverage Your Business To A Successful Transaction

You wear many hats in your business. How do you take the pulse of your business? What data do you need to make the best decisions fast? What data do you need to make your business invaluable to your clients and by extension to your prospective buyer?

Tracking And Measuring Will Make You/Your Business More Profitable

1. **Identify what numbers to follow.**

   - Sales revenue, sales volume, sales/ per project, sales/per month, sales/team member/ quotes per week, sales target/month, sales calls per day, website visitors/day, website sales/day, items sold/sale, upsells/sale, etc.

   - Profit, profit center, profit / client, profit / product, profit / campaign, profit / unit sold

   - Costs, unit costs, carrying costs, cost / unit sold, cost/campaign, cost/staff, cost/sq. ft., cost/ software seat, cost / profit center, cost/ department, direct costs, indirect costs, product defects/month, overhead

   - Marketing investments, leads generated, lead conversion, lead: sale ratios, prospects, sales calls/ sale

   - R&D investment, cost/department, cost/product, training/employee

2. **Know the Lifetime Value of Your Client**

   Define your criteria of an ideal client. Lifetime value of a basic client is $$ or $$$$:

   - Stop&Shop knows you'll come weekly and spend $50/per person

   - Macy's and Bloomingdale's ideal client comes in 4-6 times/year and spends $200/$500 each time.

   Which would you rather serve? But you can't make a good decision about which customer to market to unless you have those numbers and you track them consistently.

   If you don't track those numbers already, start now. You can use every quarter of data you amass, to add value to your business; proving it's worth every dollar you are asking for. All this tracking data is a deep resource for positioning and negotiating your exit.

Just like the imperative to have at least two years of clean financials before you are ready for an audit, you need at least two years of tracking data on your key performance indicators (KPI) to substantiate your forecast, projections and budget goals.

3. **Identify What Your Key Performance Indicators (KPI) Are:**

You must identify and track your KPI religiously.

You must be a fanatic about following these numbers. These are the numbers you receive and track in:

- Your daily reports
- Your dashboard

You already have many tools that deliver some of your KPI:

- Constant Contact
- Infusionsoft
- Google Analytics
- Your bank accounts
- Outlook
- Excel
- Access
- CRM system
- Others

What else do you need? Are there other KPI that you need from your call center, from distribution, from your merchant account? To be of value towards your exit, they must be written down and recorded in a way/form/place that create a uniform history accessible to key executives – not verbal reports, or text messages, or instant messages.

4. **Decide How to Measure**

Use whatever form or style, template or spreadsheet that works for you. Discuss and train your team on what you are tracking, what measures of change you are looking for and how these measures impact options and decisions every day. Only when you put enough value on these KPI, will your team pay attention and both deliver the data and pro-actively strive to hit better numbers.

Tracking and measuring does not have to cost anything. Use what you have already. Tracking and measuring can be:

- Manual (in-house & outsourced)
- Online (e.g., Google Docs)
- Automated (in your Contact Management software, in your operations and logistics software, in your current marketing reports)

Check what you have running. Add to your daily reports and your dashboard only those new KPI that you absolutely need in order to accelerate growth, maximize value, and make your business buyer ready.

Examples:

- Having your bookkeeper balance the books instead of you running the business out of a checkbook.
- Set up software tools that work in the background tracking everything for you.
- Implement tools or software to automate tasks so you can track and generate reports

5. **Look For Ways To Automate, Outsource & Delegate The Tracking And Measuring You Need**

The objective of tracking and measuring is not to create work for you or your team. In fact, your KPI reports should give you better and more timely data to improve decision making. My mantra is:

Delegate, Automate, Outsource
- Delegate anything that does not have to done by you
- Outsource everything possible
- Automate: reports, banking, email open/clickthrough, web analytics, appointment scheduling, systems assessments, etc.

This one discipline can transform you from a hands-on operational manager to a strategic CEO with plenty of time to work on planning and executing your exit strategy.

For example, track relevant data for each situation. Each department may be different.

1. If you pay sales people or business development people on commission, you need to track not just the % commission, but how that translates to dollars depending on the deal. If they are closing lots of small deals on a fixed price- like some list brokers – they are putting in the same hours/deal and not seeing a high returns you need.

2. If you know 1/3 of the attendees at your events buy your services, then the numbers you need to track are more likely how many prospects can you reach with your invitation and how many times do you need to reach out to them for them to attend.

3. Know your costs, before you set prices. With a client, once we tracked her true costs, not only did she radically

increase prices to a fair market value, but it was easy to ask for the new prices and clients did not quibble.

4. Use Client Relationship Management (CRM). Excel and Outlook are not CRM tools – they are good for recording data, but very limited in helping you generate the KPI for your dashboard.

What is Client Relationship Management (CRM)?

Your CRM system is about how you/your company do business with someone else/some other company. It's about nurturing the relationship between you and the customer/prospect. It gives you a 360 view to better retain every customer. CRM is a tool to cultivate relationships between people.

Effective use of your CRM system as well as the data reports it can generate for you – both add value to your business that a buyer will pay for. Keeping your CRM system up-to-date and using it for all sales, marketing and support communications provides substantive, client-specific data to back up the forecasts you use in negotiating a price for your business.

1. Choose the CRM tool that is right for your business – customize it so that it fits your company's needs/ objectives. There are many tools out there like ACT!, SageCRM, Saleslogix, MS CRM among others.

2. You have to use it to get the ROI from this tool like any other.

3. Make sure that the data in the CRM software is as up-to-date as possible – garbage in is garbage out. During due diligence, your buyer will go through this database to assess the value for themselves. Complete, accurate, accessible, and up-to-date data on your customers is a powerful tool that can measurably add value to your business.

4. The relationships are key! -Really get to know your customer so that you have a 360 degree view of their needs, likes and dislikes.

Why use a CRM system and why study the tracking and measuring reports a CRM system can generate for you?

It helps automate and streamline:

- Building your list
- Building relationships with prospects
- Keeping relationships with clients
- Integrating marketing strategies, such as
  - Email campaigns
  - A-B testing
  - Newsletters/offers/incentives
  - Telephone outreach

Tracking and measuring data can be exported from a CRM system and be used in many systems to build a strong foundation for massive growth.

Implement Plans and Systems For Results

Do you want your business to stay the size it is? Do you want to have an income stream as long as you show up each day, OR do you want to leverage what you've built into a wealth-producing machine?

To harvest all the wealth in your business, you need: Systems, Strategy, Processes, and Structure in place before you sell.

Your Business Foundation MUST have all four:

- Systems
- Strategies
- Structure
- Processes

You want to buy, train, install, and apply systems and tools that your company will not outgrow in the next 5 years. Here are benefits, steps and tools to help you get that value and demonstrate it to potential buyers.

1. **Get Organized and Get Control**
   - Track everything you do
   - Track every project
   - Review and Measure results
   - Decide what to change – only 1 thing at a time
   - Compare results

2. **Systems for Everything**
   - Immediately save $15K/yr
   - Be in control maximizing other people
   - Reporting systems
   - Automated Reports
   - Schedule everything

3. **Your Own Operations Manual**
   - Streamline what you do
   - Refine processes – fewer mistakes, omissions, more efficient, can be planned, scheduled and measured
   - Prepare for growth:
     - o Hiring, delegating, outsourcing
     - o Tools to grow
     - o Document how to execute each process, step, procedure, protocol, policy, standard, tool, and system

4. **Time Management Tools**

- 18 month strategic plan – track to plan
- Implementation calendar – measure results
- Comprehensive calendar in Outlook/Google (actual & ideal)
- Automation – to save time, save money. Look at short term cost vs. long term gain.

5. **Financial Planning Tools**

- Excel, QuickBooks, Bookkeeper, Accountant, Payroll services
- Cost analysis of each decision
- Revenue analysis of each decision
- What If Scenarios in Excel before in your checkbook

6. **Marketing Action Plans**

- Integrated tasks (event, sale, post card campaign, telephone query, social media, etc.)
- Aligned with Financial Plan
- Quantify expected results (leads, responses, qualified prospects, closes)
- Measure results - financial, time, return, quality of prospects/clients

7. **Accountability Systems**

- Schedule/Booking system
- An Assistant/Virtual Assistant
- Accountability Tools (paper, software, CDs, books)
- Board of Advisors
- Mastermind Teams
- Mentors/Advisors/Boss/Family
- Financial Reward Systems time and cash/ bonuses/ dividends

Why Don't Owners Use Tools To Track And Measure Profitability?

There are really two parallel questions

Why Don't Owners Use Tools To Track And Measure The Profitability Of Their Efforts?

Why Don't Owners Track And Measure Every Effort With Prospects And Clients?

The answers are many, wide-ranging and constant. By choice, business owners settle into a comfort zone, habits and a mindset of their own design. Without vigilance, one of the unintended consequences is a lack of tracking and measuring which can handicap or penalize the business itself. Some of the reasons can be, that owners:

- Are Too Comfortable
- Are Resistant to Change
- Assume it will be too complicated/complex even before considering options
- Presume all this is prohibitively expensive
- Are supported in their old ways that keep them out of control, overwhelmed, paralyzed, in a rut

Which ones apply to you?

Why You MUST Track & Measure in YOUR Business

The more you refine your systems, processes and procedures to improve results, tracking and measuring help you to:

- Take away stress
- Sleep at night
- Reduce mistakes
- Make better decisions easier

- Outsource/delegate any task in your business faster & cheaper when you set up systems to track and measure
- Increase efficiencies
- Get more done
- Move more off your plate
- Get more time to plan and lead
- Monetize systems, processes and procedures
- Document and monetize a wide range of intangible assets to demonstrate their value to prospective buyers

Valuation – It's More Than A Number

Valuation is the final exam giving you third party feedback and validation on what your business is worth in the market for your ideal buyer. Valuation is a measure of everything you do to accelerate growth, structure the company for growth, continuity, and acquisition. That valuation number tells you if you can sell your business for what you want out of the business, if you have already hit your number, or if you need to grow it more to be able to exit on your terms. There are many ways the business can be valued by a prospective buyer. You need to know and prepare for the valuation exercise your ideal buyer may choose.

Here are some basic methods used to calculate valuation. There are always variations.

1. **Simple Multiplier or Market Valuation**
   This method uses 'industry average' sales figure as the base for your multiple calculation. Variations of this could be average monthly gross sales, or gross sales plus inventory on hand, or net profits of comparable businesses in your industry in your region.

The catch is to find data to compare your business to. Location, outside economic factors, company size in revenue or staff or number of products, even target market niche can all add or detract from that multiplier when comparing your business to your competitors.

2. **Asset Valuation**

   The value of your business is more than what's reported on your balance sheet or in your checkbook. Asset valuation is a good fit for asset intensive retail or manufacturing businesses. You will monetize equipment, inventory at every stage, and facilities as the primary value in the business.

3. **Capitalized Earnings**

   This is the concept of valuing a business by determining its net present value (NPV) of expected future profits. In an economic sense, a company is worth the discounted amount of its net income. You can do the same thing for a specific asset (e.g., equipment), which should theoretically be worth the present value of future earnings that can be derived from it.

   This valuation method is especially appropriate for service companies and non-asset based businesses.

   The capitalization rate you use will be an estimate of the buyers risk level when investing in your business as compared with their other investment options. The capitalization rate used will be based on a variety of factors, such as:

   - How long the business has been established
   - How long you've been the owner
   - Your reasons for selling
   - Identified risk factors
   - Current profitability

- Location
- How much competition you have
- How easy or difficult is it for you to exit vs. How easy or difficult is it for others to enter your market
- Industry forecasts
- Technology you use to add value in the market
- Team contracts
- Client contracts.

The list of variables will be as long and specific as needed for your unique business.

4. **Goodwill**

   There is goodwill in every business. Goodwill consists of those intangible assets, which are identifiable non-monetary assets that cannot be seen, touched or physically measured, that are identifiable as separate assets. There are two primary forms of intangibles:

   Legal intangibles such as trade secrets (e.g., customer lists), copyrights, patents, and trademarks. Intellectual property is now often worth more than all the physical assets of the company.

   Competitive intangibles such as knowledge activities (your expertise, knowledge, experience), your collaboration activities (your team and communication), leverage activities (in your business, in your market, in your industry), and structural activities (systems, processes, structure, procedures).

5. **Return on Investment**

   Return on investment (ROI) is the most common and familiar form of business valuation. ROI is the amount of money the buyer will be able to realize from the continuing performance of the business after the sale. In this case, the focus is on the percentage the buyer will receive annually on the cash investment made to acquire the business.

Be familiar with each one and how it applies to your business and your exit goals. You need to recognize where you have leverage in negotiation by being able to demonstrate and showcase strengths and assets of your business the buyer will want to buy.

Transaction Management

When you are ready to leverage the business you have built to harvest the wealth you need for your reinvention, the preparation, organization and pace you set, will optimize the results in your favor.

Most often it is in your best interest to set your business up for a competitive transaction process. A non-competitive process will get you to a completed transaction, but you have less leverage and you give the buyer (good or bad) more control to decide the parameters of the deal.

When you do your homework early, before any buyers are on the horizon, you can keep control of the whole transaction process.

You still have many decisions to make just managing the transaction itself including:

- Timing the transaction to your timeline and the company's milestones
- Maintaining confidentiality
- When and how much to include your staff in the transaction process – or not
- When and what to communicate to your investors. You can't complete the transaction with them in the dark.

- How to market your business as a buyer ready and buyer attractive opportunity
- Transaction terms you seek/ will accept

Confidential Information Memorandum

As you prepare the business for your exit, you also need to prepare a Confidential Information Memorandum to share with prospective buyers. This is an unavoidable and critical task. It's your best marketing tool to attract ideal buyers.

Preparing a confidential information memorandum or a pitch book to sell your business will better prepare you and the business to be appealing to potential buyers. Ideally you will draft this document before a buyer comes knocking. It is your opportunity to set the tone for all follow-on discussions, setting expectations for the transaction. When a buyer is interested, this document will speed the process, increase the efficiency of the process AND strengthen overall buyer perception (increasing their valuation considerations).

You need a Confidential Information Memorandum to help potential buyers learn about your business and see the unique strategic investment opportunity it presents. Prioritize creating your Confidential Information Memorandum to share with qualified buyers because it's the most productive and efficient way to quickly assess the buyer's interest.

The effort you put in to presenting your business as professionally and attractively as possible is an investment that will pay for itself with a substantial ROI.

Just the act of preparing this Confidential Information Memorandum helps you clarify and streamline your business. Where your Exit Plan is all about you, the Confidential Information Memorandum uses the same data to build an attractive buying opportunity for qualified buyers. Your

Confidential Information Memorandum is also a valuable tool to store with your contingency plan and can be very useful in emergency situations long before your intended exit date.

Commit the resources to preparing your Confidential Information Memorandum. It may be that you hire an investment banker, an M&A advisor, or just rely on your CFO. You can't do it alone. Investment bankers and M&A advisors, even some brokers are very good at preparing this material to showcase your business in the best light to attract your ideal buyer. They can do a better job; the more you aggregate all these elements and key material and let them put together a winning package.

Here's a simplified outline of the scope of your Confidential Information Memorandum.

- Executive Summary/Introduction to the company –
- Financial Snapshot
    o Income data for the last full year and trailing 12 months
    o Balance sheet most recent reported and percentage of total assets

- Company Ownership and History
- [Narrative and Descriptive Information]
    o Industry Overview
    o Overview of the Business
    o Ownership and Control
    o History of the Business
    o Strategy and Business Model
    o Customers and Customer Relationships
    o Sales Process and/or Manufacturing Process and Capabilities
    o Products and Services
    o Market Segments

- o Competitive Overview
- o Growth Opportunities
- o Company and Product Brands
- o Sales and Communication
- o Industry Trends
- o Management Team Structure and Employees
- o Intellectual Property Overview and/or Company Assets
- o Operations and Business Process
- o Facilities and Premises
- o Vendors and Supply Chain
- o Information Systems
- o Proprietary Technology and Intellectual Property
- o Legal, Regulatory and Environmental

- Financial Performance – last 5 years
  - o Historic Income Statement Summary
  - o Historic & Adjusted EBITDA
  - o Adjusted Free Cash Flow
  - o Changes in Net Working Capital Component of Free Cash Flow

- Acquisition and Transaction Information

With your Confidential Information Memorandum in hand, you are ready for prospective buyer inquiries, giving you a stronger position from the start of your negotiations.

Transaction Process

Your transaction process can evolve over a couple years or be concentrated down to a 6 month turnaround. Regardless of the timeline, here are the basic steps to get to a deal:

1. Prepare your Confidential Information Memorandum
2. Inquiry from a potential buyer
3. Potential buyer signs an NDA (non-disclosure agreement)

4. Share your Confidential Information Memorandum with the buyer
5. A conference call after they review your Confidential Information Memorandum
   They may ask questions not just about the business directly, but also about your personal goals, your valuation number, and your ideal deal structure
6. More phone calls
7. An in-person visit to your company to tour facilities; meet your team, to get a clear picture of your business

Transaction Elements

In addition to the steps of engaging with the buyer, there are a number of elements that come in to play along the way to get the transaction closed. This is just a simple list of basic tools and documents that will be required.

- Non-Disclosure Agreement
- Confidential Information Memorandum
- Non-Binding Offer
- Due Diligence
- Binding Offer
- Exclusivity Agreement/Decision
- Structuring the Transaction
- Purchase Agreement
- Closing the Transaction

Close The Transaction – Cash Out And Get Out

It sounds obvious but it's not. Getting to the closing table with all your ducks in line and all your advisors coordinated with your buyer is a non-trivial feat of accomplishment itself. In fact, one survey of business attorneys found that only 10% of business owners ever complete the transaction to sell or pass on their business.

Preparing you and your business to get to the transaction is only Part A. Part B is concluding the transaction successfully and distributing funds to all parties engaged and involved.

But the part that gets forgotten along the way in the flurry of activity is Part C – what you do next, your reinvention and how your new liquid wealth will be applied, invested, and spent to fulfill your dreams, leave your legacy and secure your dynasty.

That's why your reinvention plan must be spelled out and documented in parallel with your exit plan. When you can clearly express what you'll be doing next: your goals, aspirations, objectives, activities and lifestyle in reinvention, then your personal advisors can set up systems, structures, vehicles in advance to protect your wealth before you receive it – so it goes where you intended without a hiccup. But your personal attorney, insurance broker, wealth advisor, and tax advisor can do very little after the fact. They can do their best work for you (at no extra cost to you) if you plan your exit early and share that plan with them. Then when they join your exit team at the table, they have all the tools in play to minimize your taxes, risk, and costs while maximizing the wealth that goes to work for you and your future.

It's up to you to communicate your goals for the business, your team and your objectives getting out.

    a. Initiate due diligence proactively. It shows potential buyers you're serious and committed to the sale. It also will identify areas, concerns, risks that can reduce your potential sale price. For example, unpaid taxes, incomplete financials, employee contract terms.

    b. Define your ultimate exit strategy, which can also uncover potential opportunities to increase or decrease the value of undocumented and unregistered intellectual property.

c. Understand the drivers inherent in a potential buyer's business. Put yourself in that buyer's shoes to take a critical look at your own business. If you skip this step or minimize it, you risk leaving money on the table.

ACHIEVE

Is Retirement the Same as Death?

Entrepreneurs in the US for the most part are stuck. They are working hard long hours to create an income stream. If they stop working, there's no income.

The fallacy is that there is no exit, and never will be, if you only focus on generating an income stream to pay your salary or to meet payroll. Without a wealth plan in place, a wealth plan established from profits, then retirement might as well be death because those same hardworking owners have no assets to walk away with, no assets to invest for their future.

When I talk to some owners and the subject of retirement comes up – you would think I was talking about their mortality. They equate any form of leaving the business as death. They live for the business. They have become so immersed in the business; they've lost sight of the purpose of commercial enterprise, their commercial enterprise.

The purpose of all commerce is to make a profit. When an owner can turn a profit and exit on their terms and timeline, that's a successful business and a successful exit.

My assumption is that every owner wants to liquidate their position in the company they built/own at some point, whether to fund their next step, even if it's not a classic retirement; secure the future for their family and loved ones; or fulfill the terms of a will or trust. Even those owners who resist planning their exit, often procrastinate because they don't know what to do or how to do it. No one intends to leave their business feet first without a plan for its continued success; but in epidemic proportions, they just don't initiate and implement a timely exit plan.

When an owner can walk away from the business with liquidity to fund their reinvention on their terms for three or four more decades, instead of a rocking chair, knitting needles or fishing pole; that's not retirement or death. That's freedom and financial independence. You can too.

Seven Keys to Success

Keep these intangible keys to success in mind as you persist to harvest your wealth.

1. **Awareness:** It's important to know who you are, how you got here, and what kind of decisions you're making. We all get *programmed* as kids, but that doesn't mean we have to live our whole lives with that programming.

2. **Vision:** Imagine the details of the life you want to live. We each make our own roadmap – consciously or unconsciously – and having a vision lets us know where we are going.

3. **Purpose:** Understand why you want to get to the destination (reinvention). There's more to life than hard work and grubbing after money. Finding purpose in everything you do puts a fulfilling life and legacy within your grasp.

4. **Belief:** We all believe in ourselves to some extent. Increasing that personal belief – your confidence – is a major component for being able to move forward.

5. **Action:** There are different types of action we take based on our awareness, vision, purpose, and belief. The momentum we build with our actions serves to propel our growth and development.

6. **Gratitude:** This is a deep and personal thing. I'm thankful every day for my parents, siblings and sons.

Being able to have gratitude for what we have in life – no matter where we're at – is the hallmark of success.

7. **Forgiveness:** This is the hidden key to achieving and **keeping** success. Setting aside "what has happened" in favor of "what can be" means you'll have your hands free to hold your success when it comes.

Transition to Your Reinvention

If exiting your business does not need to lead to retirement and death, what's the alternative? It's your choice, both because you're the exiting owner and because your opportunity is not your parents' retirement expectations.

What's next can and should be your reinvention.

Our parents worked 9-5 jobs for large companies with a pension and retirement benefits built into their compensation package. They were loyal to the company for 20, 30 or more years and were rewarded with a secure pension to rest and relax for the rest of their lives.

That model has all but been wiped out. In its place every working individual has to plan, save, and invest over a lifetime of jobs, career moves and other changes to create the wealth to provide financial independence. As the owner of your business, you have been working long hours for many years to build the business to provide an income, while benefiting from and enjoying some tax-advantaged benefits of ownership (e.g., company paid and/or tax deductible health insurance, use of a company car, paid vacations, etc.).

When you sell or pass on your business, many of those benefits become expenses instead of deductions if you want to maintain the same lifestyle.

Your reinvention in the 21st century will look very different from your parents' retirement. Some general observations:

1. The actuarial tables for the second half of the 20th century forecast life expectancy to be retirement + 3 years.
2. Our parents left a job or career to go home and read, knit, cook, play golf or play with the grandchildren.
3. There was no expectation they would pursue gainful employment, start new businesses, or make major contributions as 'old, retired' people.
4. They were sidelined by society.

None of that is true for today's Baby-Boomer business owners, the primary audience for this book. As Baby-Boomers, we:

1. Expect to live decades into the retirement years
2. Have the health, vitality, wisdom and creativity to reinvent ourselves, our lives and start over if we want to
3. Have no intention of retiring by any definition
4. Have more plans for the next three, four or more decades of our lives
5. Have the wealth, financial independence and education to expand our options and choices in reinvention.
6. Are choosing and planning our reinvention to be some combination of:

   a. **a new venture** – for profit or not, a spinoff of the business just sold, or something entirely new – whether the liquidity from the exit transaction will be used to fund it or not
   b. **an adventure** – whether that means moving to the coast, to the mountains, to a resort community, to a

55+ community, or moving to Panama, Belize or Singapore, or sailing around the world for a year

c. **an avocation** – a cause or organization to contribute more time and resources to

d. **a hobby** – whether it's learning golf, a musical instrument, or a new language or spending more time on an activity you love like horseback riding, scuba diving, sailing or skiing.

You must plan your transition to reinvention in the same systematic way you approach the sale of your business. One is closing out a chapter of your life. The other is setting up, structuring and preparing for the next chapter of your life. It is essential that these two projects progress in tandem to achieve a smooth handoff from one to the other when you exit your business.

PART IV
Maximizing Profits Solution

You **can** exit your business on your terms so you can transition to the lifestyle of your dreams with the wealth to pursue your reinvention (venture, adventure, avocation, hobby, retirement). What you **can't** do is assume you can simply hire a team of experts and walk away from your business in the next six months.

Below is a brief outline of the scope of planning to address early. The more completely you define and document each element below, the stronger and clearer will be your exit blueprint, whether you execute it in three years or three decades. Engage an exit strategist to keep you focused and help you integrate these decisions and plans into your current operational objectives and lifestyle.

Exit Criteria

Start with your exit criteria to achieve your ultimate goals.

- **Freedom** – what does freedom look like to you when you exit your business?
- **Flexibility** – What is your definition of flexibility when you think about how you exit, the terms of your exit or what you can and cannot do after the exit transaction is complete?
- **Control** – Who's in control of decisions, strategy, budget, operations, and sales now? Who will be in

control of each area of the business when you exit? Have you transitioned the decisions and control to one person, to a team of leaders or to no one leaving a vacuum in the business?

- **Wealth** – What is your wealth requirement for your reinvention and lifestyle after you exit? How do you define wealth? How much of the wealth you need for your reinvention must come from the business? Can you liquidate the business to produce that level of wealth to achieve your other exit criteria?

- **Liquidity** – How much liquidity do you need immediately when you exit? How long can you wait to receive final payment?

- **Timeline** – What is your ideal timeline for your exit? for your reinvention? for liquidity?

- **Legacy** – What's your definition of the legacy you want to leave behind? What do you and your business stand for? What do you want to be remembered for? How can you achieve that?

- **Dynasty** – Do you want to build a family dynasty? What would that look like? What do you have to put in place to realize your dynasty?

Exit Planning

Ideally, exit planning occurs before action in every area.

Business owners are often surprised by how extensive the planning is that they must work through before they can get out, including:

- **Exit Objectives** – Before you proceed, you must identify your exit objectives for the business and for your life beyond the exit.

- **Value Drivers** – You must identify your value drivers; the value drivers that will make the business buyer attractive, secure the future growth of the business, and protect your employees.
- **Transfer Control/ Ownership/ Management** – These three things are not the same. Planning how to transfer these different skill sets to successors is essential.
- **Contingency Planning** – If illness or an accident incapacitates you, your valuation will plummet unless you have your contingency plan/continuity plan already in place.
- **Wealth Management/Preservation** – Decide how much of the illiquid wealth of your business to leave in the business to maximize valuation and secure future company success vs. how much you need to liquidate for financial freedom and your reinvention.
- **Successful Exit** – It's unique to you, your family, your goals, your business, and the lifestyle of your dreams. If you can't describe it, you will never know when the package a prospective buyer puts on the table meets your needs.
- **Exit Options** – The earlier you start exit planning, the more options you have; and the wider range of wealth vehicles and reinvention options you have.

Exit Options

There are tradeoffs for every exit strategy you consider. The chart below may be useful in exploring which options you want to consider. Your exit can be as unique as the business you've built, the team that surrounds you, your core values and culture; and your leadership.

Exit Option Table

Exit Options	Definition	Seller Benefits	Seller Drawbacks
Merger with another company	Your company joins with an existing company.	You may receive cash and/or stock. Resources of the two companies are combined. Some of your management team may be kept on.	The new owner/ manager may have different ideas of how to run the business. Your existing team may not have the control they had under your leadership. Merging the two cultures may be challenging.
Acquisition by another company	Your company is bought out by another existing company.	You may receive cash and/or stock for the sale. You may be required to stay on in some capacity for a specified period of time for transition.	Your corporate brand and identity may or may not be preserved. The fit may not be perfect for the business or your team.
Sale to a Strategic Buyer	A strategic buyer who wants to run the company buys you out.	You may receive cash immediately or structured over a set timeline.	It can be difficult to find the right buyer, at the right price on your schedule. Changing ownership or management may be difficult for employees and management.
Sale to a Financial Buyer	A financial buyer who wants to add your company to their portfolio of managed companies	You may receive cash immediately or structured over a set timeline. You may be required to stay on in some capacity for a specified period of time for transition.	Financial buyers are looking at the numbers and how to get a good return on their investment. How they do that may be difficult for employees, management and clients. There may be a clash of culture and values.
Franchise the Company	If your business is replicable, this allows you to expand locally, regionally, even internationally.	You receive cash from each franchisee. Your current management team and structure are maintained. Franchising is an opportunity for large-scale growth	Franchising takes time. The process can be difficult and time –consuming. Not every business is suitable for franchising

Exit Options	Definition	Seller Benefits	Seller Drawbacks
Employee Stock Ownership Plan (ESOP)	Employees earn/accrue shares or stock of the company over time.	Employees are rewarded for contributions, receive incentives for longevity and share in the profits of the company they helped you grow.	Employees may lose their shares if they leave the company, employees share the burden and risk if the value of the company goes down.
Management Buyout	Some or all of the existing management team buyout the owner. This is one version of a group buying the company instead of an individual strategic buyer.	You may receive cash immediately or structured over a set timeline. You may stay on in some capacity for a specified period of time for transition.	Managers may not agree on how to run the business without your leadership. Negotiating a transaction may include many more factors and conditions, as the buyers are also the team being valued.
Initial Public Offering (IPO)	Shares of the company are sold publically on a stock exchange.	Shares convert to cash for the owner and any initial investors. Major shareholder control the company. Investors expect to see a high return on their investment	The company must deliver high growth to generate earnings and interest for investors, IPO costs are very high. IPOs offer a very uncertain outcome for owners or investors.
Succession	Someone inside the company, inside the family or hired in is trained and groomed to succeed the owner	You handpick your successor on your terms	You are dependent on the effectiveness of your successor to ensure the company can pay you (cash, annuity, payment schedule) and sustain the company moving forward.
Close the Doors	Cease operations and liquidate assets	Minimize losses, quick exit. Common decision of families if you die with no contingency plan or transition.	Without any effort to monetize revenue streams or intellectual property, you eliminate any chance to profit from the business.

Exit Strategy Stages

An exit plan to sell your business is more than a transaction. When you understand that there are five stages to the exit process and that there is a systematic way to move through the whole process without getting overwhelmed or discouraged, you can relax and simply 'work the process'. That's what these five exit strategy stages are all about.

- Exploration/Evaluation – This is where all your exit planning happens to understand the scope of work to do, the opportunities and timeline involved to achieve your exit to reinvention.

- Growth Process Implementation – To maximize the value of the business and build a deep foundation to make the business buyer attractive, you need to put a growth strategy into motion. If you sell the business as is, the buyers can't see the future value to them in what you do now.

- Exit Integration – The exit transaction is the culmination of all your planning, preparing the business and your team for your exit, maximizing value and determining the kind of exit you want and the terms you want to exit, along with the terms, timeline, cashflow for your reinvention.

  But you can't plan or execute on your exit in isolation. You must also keep a finger on the pulse of your business, in terms of growth, accelerating sales and grooming successors to add value and make it extremely buyer attractive.

- Track& Measure for Excellence & Value – Tracking and measuring are the only way you ever know if you are getting the results you want. Tracking and measuring also help you raise the bar and add value in the intellectual property you own and the goodwill value you've built up in the business. Tracking and measuring is an essential toolkit you must employee, refine and promote to buyers to demonstrate your team and business excellence and the value they are worth independent of you, your presence or your leadership.

- Implement the Transition to Reinvention - Only when you pull it all together and get to the closing table for an exit transaction can you move forward with the financial freedom to fulfill your reinvention plan. Only when you have a reinvention plan are you ready to come to the closing table. Make sure the two are aligned so you achieve an exit strategy for wealth.

We're At The End, But, That's Not All Folks

Is It Possible To Achieve Both Business And Personal Goals In Exit Planning?

Without planning and forethought, your personal and business goals for the outcome of any exit may be in conflict. To achieve business and personal goals in parallel, here are a few core strategies to use:

Document Your Exit Plan – to include the growth strategies that will maximize valuation on your timeline. Get the plan out of your head. This will make it tangible and real for everyone. It takes the decisions to be made out of the realm of emotions and dreams and turns them into concrete actionable tasks.

Protect And Maintain The Value Of The Business that you can monetize at exit. Minimize the risk that any growth strategy you invoke will negatively impact the growth curve you are forecasting for the buyers.

Train and Delegate Move key employees into positions of operational responsibility and reward them for results. When you both train and delegate, you add immediate value to the employees directly, motivate them to stay and demonstrate to buyers that the value is in the business, not in you, the exiting owner.

Evaluate All Your Primary Exit Options (financial or strategic sale, employee or management buyout, transferring ownership within the family) thoroughly, not just to fulfill your dreams but also to ensure the ongoing success of the business and job security of your employees from the growth trajectory you've put in place.

Activate Your All-star Team Seek out and build a powerful team of experts, multi-disciplinary advisors to help you achieve your goals. Whether your business value is $2M or $50M, you'll face the same issues along the way. Start with an exit strategist who can look at the whole business, not just the exit transaction right through to implementing your next steps, your reinvention after a successful exit. Your exit strategist should be a masterful quarterback and facilitator for your team of experts, allowing you to focus on building value in the business.

What's Next?

I am pleased and honored to: contribute to the discussion going on in your head, ignite more confidence, competence and possibility thinking, inspire you to greater strategic planning and more leadership initiative and enable any entrepreneur or owner to exit their business by achieving every goal they set. Which I hope this book has accomplished.

Now that you've read *HARVEST Your Wealth - Exit Essentials for Your Business©*, if I did my job you're not exactly the same business thinker you were on page one. You should see at least the beginnings of the expansive, non-linear, 360°, 10,000 foot view I want you to embrace. You should now be thinking not about what you can't accomplish, but of what you CAN accomplish in your business and beyond and what is honestly and significantly possible to fulfill your dream on your terms, on your timeline.

I hope you have, at minimum, the urgency of forcing yourself out of your everyday comfort zone that produces more of the same old ideas, old solutions, and tired results; and into more, extensive, 3-dimensional thinking. Hopefully your thinking is more expansive, more creatively oriented and you're looking at your business, competition and exit opportunities from a position that is brilliantly open-minded, inspired and all encompassing. If I've succeeded at all introducing you to exit essentials, you've opened a window into a sense of much greater possibility to formulate a plan to harvest the wealth in your business on your terms, on your timeline.

The Sun Never Sees A Shadow

Think of the most successful business leaders you know. They are never idle. They don't stand still. They are always moving forward. They don't look for problems and opportunities just from one angle. They keep moving and view their business from all directions. They see the shadows and explore what's hidden in those shadows. To accelerate growth and maximize value, they seek out and find new solutions and get meaningful, life-changing results that their competition never will. In every decision they make, they are always asking is this decision taking me closer or pulling me away from my long-term plan to sell/scale or find a successor.

Obviously, there's much more to learn and much more that can be achieved to make your business a wealth producing machine that allows you to transition to your reinvention, fulfill promises and walk away with the financial freedom to live the life of your dreams.

I can help you get there faster, sooner. I can make the job easier, and far more enriching for you if you're interested in my personal assistance.

A Way I Might Be Able to Help You More Directly

If you're company is large enough, if you're open minded enough, if you're committed to maximizing the value in the business to produce more wealth for you, and if you're excited about the possibility of making the shift to doing more, solving more, winning more, and succeeding more; there might be a way I can be more directly involved in guaranteeing your future dreams come true.

There are many ways I work with clients:

- Personal Advisory Relationships – Mentoring, Not Coaching
- Customized Business Relationships To Fit Your Strategic/Exit Needs
- 1 Day Fee-Based
- 12 Month program to Build Your Business Value
- Long Term, Minimal Retainer Fee with Percentage Contingency on Exit. Only applies to solid businesses currently doing 7-8 figures or more.

I bring the most value to your business and your ultimate wealth, when we build a long-term relationship. It won't be worthwhile if I'm bamboozling you, or I drop the ball or you hate my guts. I would have nothing to gain there and everything to lose. I am more long-term oriented rather than a rush at the end.

When you wait until the last six months before you want to get out to start thinking about how to get your money out of the business, or to figure out what it's worth, or more importantly how much money you need out of the business to move on to your next venture, travel, avocation or hobby, here's what happens:

1. You have fewer choices
2. Your valuation will be lower
3. You have less time/options to make the business buyer attractive
4. You leave 30-50% of the value of the business on the table
5. The buyer holds all the cards
6. Much harder to complete a transaction that produces your financial freedom
7. You and the business take a bigger tax hit
8. The business may not survive the transaction
9. The buyer will limit the cash you get out up front
10. The buyer will require your participation, expertise for an extended period of time
11. You risk walking away with not enough to fund your reinvention dream
12. Your reinvention plan has not been tested and you don't have the next 365 days booked solid.
13. Your wealth advisor is ill-prepared to maximize your wealth to ensure your financial future.
14. Your tax advisors and attorneys don't have your affairs structured to protect you best

So your challenge is to grow the business, add value to the business and make the business buyer ready before you implement your contingency plan, succession plan, or transition plan.

"The difference between greatness and mediocrity, mediocrity and millions, spectacular and pathetic performance is how well you use your time, your opportunities, your efforts, your resources and your assets." Jay Abraham

---

Most entrepreneurs know they can make a good **income** running their business day-to-day, but SOME OWNERS INSTINCTIVELY know that their **real payday** will come only when they exit the business, most likely sell the business.

That's when they can access multiple millions of dollars from their business.

1. Is this something you have thought about?
2. Do you want your business to produce a multi-million dollar windfall?
3. Do you think it's possible for <u>your</u> business to fund a multi-million dollar reinvention for you?
4. Do you know how much your business is worth right now?
5. 95% of all business owners do not have an exit plan – because most owners don't know what their business is worth. As a result, most owners are walking away with only 50-70% of what their business is worth.

Sadly, most owners and entrepreneurs fail to achieve their dream and get out the way they want to just because of a lack of planning, and forethought. It's totally preventable.

Only owners who invest the time, effort and expertise to plan their exit and make their business appealing to **buyers** are among the **5%** who achieve their dream and the lifestyle it offers.

Every business owner has three OPTIONS of how they'll get out:

1. **The first option is the default that over 95% of all business owners choose –** That's to do nothing, exit feet first and leave your family to liquidate the business as best they can to pay estate taxes.
2. **The standard option** is to pay a fee ($50K+)and commission (3-10%) upon sale with an outcome that can

pay you the owner just two to three times the operating profit six to ten years from now.

Have you thought about this as a viable option?
Is that the return you were looking for?
Can you finance your reinvention on that?
Is it close to your Number?
Are you aware of how this works?

I'd like to make sure you know about it – but I think it's a rotten option that favors the buyer. But you need to know what it is – to know how distasteful it is for you.

But did you know it's in your better interest to exit early, that when you exit in the first three to five years your ROI is greater? And if you exit in the <u>next</u> five years (2013 – 2018), it is optimal timing to take advantage of the seller's market, instead of competing in the buyer's market if you wait more than 5 years (beyond 2018).

3. I offer a **3rd option** for how to get out. My new Exit Framework paradigm is more pro-active and measurably more expensive up front. My approach helps owners optimize and leverage results early. They exit two to four years earlier for a likely higher multiple of an improved EBITA (operating profit), instead.

Your Choices

- Take my third option and get out years earlier, with four to six times EBITA on potentially higher revenues, in cash, with systems, structures and wealth preserving vehicles in place to maintain the lifestyle and benefits your business has provided, or

- Take the standard option of two-to four times EBITA six to ten years from now with an earn-out commitment, in an even more competitive buyer's market.

Here's how I make you succeed. I take a comprehensive strategic approach with only one objective, to help you the selling business owner get out on your terms on your timeline. This is all I do.

Now let me tell you a bit about how we work.

I'm a specialist in engineering how you harvest the wealth out of your business. I'm an expert on preparing you, your company and your team for your exit to achieve your dreams. I've been hired by corporate leaders, fast-track entrepreneurs, royalty, family businesses, and multi-millionaires, among others.

In one company, when we cleaned up the financials to understand true costs, we doubled prices three times in six months with no impact on the backlog of orders. As a result, the owner is finally running a profitable operation, taking a more strategic role, wearing fewer hats, taking time off and executing her plan for a profitable exit.

In another company, we planned the owner's exit as part of the launch. Growth, market demand, and expansion are accelerating. She is almost 2 years ahead of schedule on her $5M exit timeline.

In a $4M startup, we built the contingency plan and the operational plan alongside the business plan, knowing the owner's MS could put the operation at risk at any time.

In a young e-commerce startup, the owner came to me less than 6 months into opening their doors, to structure the business to achieve her growth and valuation goals, to secure her retirement.

The founder of a $6M startup came to me when he wanted to develop his exit plan before he finalized the corporate strategy for the investors. By defining his end game as part of the business plan, he now ties every short-term and mid-term goal to his long-term objectives.

Most experts and advisors who provide exit planning have one or both of the following:

1. **They have financial credentials** (CPA, CFP, Investment licenses, Insurance licenses, tax certifications, etc.) and offer exit planning as an add-on service. Their strength and focus is on your financials. Some work for you personally. Some work for your business. Some look at both.

   With a business that's grown to millions if not tens of millions, you've learned that your accountant and your CFO have different roles within your business and it's often short-sighted to ask one person to wear both hats.

   The same can be said when you ask an accountant, attorney, broker, wealth advisor or tax advisor about exit planning. Their strength is to see the world through the lens of their expertise. In the case of working on how to get out of the business, their toolkit does not include all the tools you may need that we covered here.

2. **They work for or get paid by the buyer for a successful transaction**. Brokers, investment bankers and M&A advisors may take a fee from you the seller to cover certain services up front, but their payday is at the closing.

   When they do their due diligence, they'll tell you what you need to do to fix things, to increase valuation, etc., to be buyer ready; but they don't stick around to help you do it. Rather, they give you a punch list for you to figure out and act on fast, all while still running the company day to day. They too are all about the numbers.

Notice – *their primary focus is not on preparing you the owner, your business or your team for the transaction in the years leading up to that milestone event. They are transaction driven and work for closure.*

They don't get paid to help you the owner maximize the value of your business before the transaction.

They don't get into the business fundamentals, the growth strategies, cleaning up the financials, contingency planning, protecting intellectual property, employee contracts to tie the team to the company beyond your departure, succession planning, protecting and preserving your wealth goals, minimizing both your tax concerns and the company's tax impact, your personal transition or your reinvention.

Indeed, they are your trusted advisors. And for a fee, they'll also work with you on these things outside their experience and expertise. But it's not their primary bailiwick.

The data proves that this approach is failing you, the owner. Only a dismal 10% of all sellers (business owner like you) EVER close the deal, and complete the transaction.

It takes at least two to five years to prepare you, your team and your business to transition to what's next, profitably. These expert advisors don't always take a 360^0 view, help execute, or look that far ahead.

I do.

Qualifying Questions To Ask Anyone You Want To Consider As Your Exit Planning Virtual Partner

1. **What is your specialty? What is your core business?**

   You want an exit strategist whose focus is exclusively on your optimal exit, who is not distracted by other disciplines.

2. **How will you charge me for exit planning services pre and post transaction?**

   You want to know you are being charged for exit planning expertise and exit planning time, not attorney time to do exit planning. You need an exit strategist on board, engaged in your situation years before you need your attorneys, accountants, and wealth and insurance advisors.

3. **How engaged will you be in my operational implementation and transition up to the transaction?**

   Leading up to the transaction, licensed advisors will be focused on the expertise they bring to the table. Their availability will be limited to help you with operational decisions and issues leading up to the transaction. After the transaction, you will need your exit strategist engaged to ensure your total integration into your reinvention lifestyle, but after the transaction, licensed expert advisors will move on to the next transaction. How much will they/can they be there for you?

   You want an exit planner who will be fully engaged in operational implementation, growth and optimization strategies and your own transformation from operational president/owner to the strategic CEO of a stronger more profitable enterprise, not just the six-month end game.

4. **Will you help me assess exit options and timing/ tax/liquidity impact of each?**

   You need an exit planner to help facilitate discussions with all your exit advisors to integrate their recommendations and tradeoffs for each exit option you are considering. An exit expert who stays focused in their own silo of expertise cannot provide the wider perspective you need to make the best decisions.

5. **What will you do to assist me in determining my reinvention plan and my goals and lifestyle beyond the business exit?**

   The licensed experts you engage for their expertise can ask you all the right questions, but they expect you to prepare and deliver the answers on your own. You need an exit strategist who will assist you in developing your reinvention plan and lifestyle beyond the exit, test it, refine it and lay out a blueprint to implement it from Day 1 of your reinvention.

Whether you work with me or not, you need to use the materials, checklists, tables and guidelines provided here in *HARVEST Your Wealth – Exit Essentials for Your Business,* to make your business a wealth producing machine that will provide the financial independence you dream of to fund your reinvention.

If you have interest in working with me, and your business fits my client requirements, I'd very much like to talk with you. Exploring options and opportunities is always a worthwhile process for both sides. It broadens each other's mindset to how much more might be possible and in how many more ways we could accomplish that!

Please call my office at **508.820.3322** during business hours in Massachusetts or contact me at **exploreoptions@thiswayoutgroup.com** .

To engage me personally, your access to my personal services/programs requires the ability both financially and operationally, to capitalize on what I would share and to implement, execute, and apply my ideas, strategies and recommendations to achieve your optimal exit.

There are no limits. I know that, I've seen that. I've made it happen. And I want you to experience the same exceptional life changing results.

If you know there's measurable value in the assets you've created and you want to unlock that value for a multi-million dollar payday, you need to start now.

Would you rather procrastinate on your dream or get started today?

Stay Connected

Stay connected with me:

Twitter –@Kerri Salls

Facebook – http://facebook.com/ThisWayOutGroup

Author Website – http://kerrisalls.com

Business Website - http://thiswayoutgroup.com

Exit Framework Blog – http://thiswayoutgroup.com/blog

URBusinessNetwork – http://urbusinessnetwork.com
Internet business radio network where I host the daily show:
Exit This Way

Other Publications

Exit This Way Ebook series [www.amazon.com date: TBD]

How to Manage a Gaggle of Advisors to Build Your All-Star Exit Team [http://thiswayoutgroup.com]

Don't Murder Your Business [http://thiswayoutgroup.com]

www.ingramcontent.com/pod-product-compliance
Lightning Source LLC
Chambersburg PA
CBHW060538210326
41519CB00014B/3255